Just A Dumb Kid From Nowhere

ISBN: 978-0-9845926-5-4
Library of Congress Control Number: 2010939663
Published by Global Authors Publications

Filling the GAP in publishing

Edited by Lynn Thompson
Interior Design by KathleenWalls
Cover Design by Kathleen Walls

Printed in USA for Global Authors Publications

Just A Dumb Kid From Nowhere

Joe Abb Overby

Dedication:

For my late brother, Dub,who took care of me when I was young and had no one else to lean on.

Also for the Methodist Orphans Home in Jackson, Mississippi for taking me into their care when I was 3 years and 8 months old. God only knows what would have happened to me if they were not there for young children like myself.

Acknowledgements:

Many thanks to Lynn Thompson at Thompson Writing & Editing (www.thompsonwriting.com) for helping me polish up this story into a manuscript suitable for publishing, for enhancing it with historical research, and for passing along information and advice on the publishing and marketing processes.

Foreword:

This is the story of my life, up to about the age of fourteen. Parts of it still make me emotional to think about, and I hope that they move you, as well.

People who have been with their mothers all their lives can never feel the pain and understand how troubling it is for children who don't have this. If you had a loving mother who put you to bed at night, or a loving grandmother, or even a loving relative who touched you and tucked you in at night with a loving hug and a kiss, go to them and tell them to read this book. Tell them you love them with all your heart and thank God you never had to go through the lonely nights like the kids in an orphans' home do.

The quest for my mother was a large part of my younger childhood. This must be instinct for a young child to continue to search for his mother when she leaves him.

I hope that my story touches you, makes you laugh and cry, and brings a new appreciation for the family who loves you.

-Joe Overby

Chapter 1
Sheriff Shootin'

There's nothing like the blast of a twelve-gauge shotgun to cut through the idyll of a three-year-old boy's day.

I was sitting in my older brother's lap in the front yard, eating cornbread and milk. A car was parked just outside the picket fence around our yard, with the county sheriff and two of his deputies standing around its open doors. The car was relatively new, a black two-seater, maybe twice as old as I was. When the sheriff and his men saw my father come out of the house with the shotgun, they quickly took cover behind the car and drew their pistols. "Don't shoot, Bill! Please, please, don't shoot!"

My dad leveled his twelve-gauge, pointed toward the sheriff's car and fired away. The bowl of cornbread and milk went flying as I jumped down and started running around the grassless front yard, screaming and hollering.

Buckshot went all over the place, but the only one who got hit was the sheriff. One buckshot went through his left earlobe. Dad walked over to the porch, laid down the shotgun and yelled to the sheriff, "You sumbitch! That's for screwin' my wife while I was at the café, working!"

We lived in a nice little farmhouse with a picket fence around it, just outside the small town of Reform, Mississippi. My father, Bill Overby, was co-owner of a little hotel and café in town, just across from the train depot. My mother, Candace, stayed at the farmhouse with us kids. She and my oldest brother, Dub, raised vegetables for the café, and my father came out to get them two nights a week. The rest of the time, he lived in town.

That's how the trouble started, really. You see, my mother was only seventeen when she married Dad. He'd already had one family, up in Bruce, and had deserted them to be with her. That made him in his fifties, and her only seventeen, when they got married. My mother couldn't read or write, and her mother had died young. Before my dad came along, she'd lived with her father, who couldn't read or write, either. He'd just worked odd jobs while she cooked and washed for him, just like she did for us. As for us kids, there was my oldest brother Dub, who was four years older than me, middle brother John, eighteen months older than me, and me, Joe—or, as everybody called me "Joe Abb." I was three years and some months old at this time.

1

It was actually me who'd given Dub his name. Before I'd come along, everybody called him by his initials, which were W.J. It was a common practice in Mississippi at that time to call people by their initials. When I was first learning to talk, I could only say "duh-duh-duh-Dub-uh-jay." Thus, Dub acquired his name for life.

None of us knew this at the time, but a couple hours before the shooting incident, my father had just beaten my mother. Dub told me later on that was a regular occurrence. She'd walked about a mile down the dirt road to the neighbor's house to call the sheriff. They had the only phone within two miles. She would run down there whenever he beat her, and this time the neighbor had insisted on calling the sheriff.

After my father laid the shotgun down, the sheriff and his deputies moved in. "Dangitall, Bill, you done gone and shot me!" said the sheriff, holding his bloodied earlobe. "Now you *know* I got to take you in."

I was still running around, and had made it to the back yard before Dub caught me. I seem to remember my mother being back there, too. The sheriff arrested Dad and the car drove off with him in the back seat.

They booked him in the County Jail, down in Ackerman. Dub told us he was charged with "A&B to Kill," which was the official legal term in rural Mississippi at that time for assault & battery with the intention of murder.

Now, Dad was usually a likeable guy. At a younger age, he'd been very handsome, and all the ladies had thought he was quite the guy. I always knew him as an old man, since he was close to 60 years old when I was born. One of my aunts told me in later years that Dad was carrying on with other women in town, just like the sheriff was doing with my mother. "He had other women his whole life," she said, "but he didn't want your mother to have anyone else but him."

Dub was closer to our mother than John or I were. When we were all middle-aged, Dub said to me one day, "She was seventeen years old and married a 52-year-old man she could not relate to. She really had no mother and no smarts. She did the best she could do during the Depression years and the sawmill boom in the poor-ass state of Mississippi. So, Joe, don't say anything bad about my mother." I got the impression Dub knew a lot more than he was telling me, even with that much time having passed.

Dad stayed in jail until the trial. Nobody bailed him out. He didn't have a dime, and he owed money on the farm, the hotel and the café. All of that was about to be taken over by the mortgage holder.

By the time Dad's trial came around, everybody in the area turned out for it. You couldn't get a seat in the courthouse. Of course, they wouldn't let us kids into the courtroom, but Dub found out what was going on from people who had been there. He pulled us together to tell us about it. "Y'all, there's lots of winkin' and whisperin' and snickerin' goin' on, all over the county."

"Why, Dub?" asked John.

"Because everybody knows what's been going on 'tween the sheriff and our momma."

"The sheriff an' Momma? What you sayin', Dub?"

Back in the 1930's, all the men in rural Mississippi used to go fox hunting. This was a great sport, and still is today. Fox hunting is done at night, when a group of men get together and take their foxhounds out on a lonely dirt road, build a fire and turn the dogs loose. While the hounds are running, looking for foxes, the men sit around the fire, drink homemade moonshine whiskey and chew tobacco. They all listen for the "turkey chop" bark, which will mean that their dog has found a fox.

Sometimes the men would find other ways to kill the time. We lived on a lonely dirt road, so the area around our farm was popular for fox hunting. The county sheriff had taken a liking to my mother, and would come by the house to call on her while his dogs were out running foxes. She'd sneak outside and meet him in the moonlight. John and I were too young to understand this at the time, but Dub explained it to us as best he could. He remembered hearing the "oohs" and "aahs" outside the house while they thought we were all asleep.

So, my mother had been carrying on with the county sheriff while Dad was in town. That was what my father had found out that had made him beat my mother and shoot at the sheriff.

"It sounds pretty bad for Dad," Dub told us. "You know where that big ol' oak tree blowed over and left that big hole in the ground?"

"Yeah?"

"Well, Dad also shot a couple of the sheriff's hound dogs and buried 'em in that hole." In that part of Mississippi, shooting a man's fox hound was just as bad as sleeping with his wife, both then and now. "That's why the sheriff and them deputies come out here that day. They was gonna arrest Dad for shootin' them dogs."

"Ohhh. Not for beatin' up Momma?"

"Naw, they don't care nothin' about that."

In the end, my father was found guilty and sentenced to eight years in the state penitentiary at Parchman. Everything we had at the time was taken from us, and we were left homeless and penniless.

Turbulent as that day may have been, living in that little farmhouse, with a fire in the fireplace, food on the table and nice clothes to wear, would prove to be one of the most peaceful times in my young life. The hard times were just beginning.

Chapter 2
The Price of Betrayal

In the following weeks, I don't have many memories of what happened to us. Dub told me later that we'd live someplace for a week or so, then get kicked out and find some other place. We were hungry, dirty, no clothes, no shoes, living mostly in vacant farmhouses and shacks all over the county.

None of my mother's former lovers would acknowledge her. They were all married, and now that everybody in the county knew what had been going on, they were embarrassed to be associated with her. Helping us would have acknowledged that they knew her, so none of them did. To make matters worse, she was going to have another baby soon. Because my dad had beaten her, the state gave her an automatic divorce when he was sent to prison. I was the youngest, so I didn't understand any of this, but Dub explained it all to me, best as he could.

Finally, toward the end of June, the sheriff and another man put us all in the back seat of his car and drove us down to Jackson, the state capitol. Dub was sitting closest to the door on the right-hand side, then my mother, then me, then John next to the door on the left-hand side, behind the driver. I'd never been to the state capitol before, so I was kind of excited.

It was mid-afternoon by the time we reached our destination. We stopped somewhere just outside the city, and parked in front of a huge building. I'd never seen a building that big before. "Momma, is this the state capitol?" I asked. She didn't say a word. There was a lot of whispering going on in the car, and something about it made me uneasy. I started holding on to my mother and would not let go.

We sat there for some time, and nobody got out of the car. Something just didn't seem right to me. After what seemed like forever, a young girl came out of the building, and came over to the car. She was quite pretty, and started playing little games with me. She said, "I know where there's a box of candy, and if you come with me, you can have all you want."

I just looked at her.

She smiled and said, "I found the candy at the end of the rainbow. Please don't tell nobody else, and it'll all belong to you."

"I'll go if my two brothers and my mother can go, too," I said.

"Only you and your brothers can go. We'll bring the whole box back to your mother."

A whole box of candy, just for me? And we could bring it back to my mother? That was too good for me to pass up. "Okay," I finally said. John and I followed her inside, but Dub stayed behind, still clinging to our mother.

As soon as we got inside the door, it slammed shut behind us. The girl disappeared, and I started crying and hollering. John later told me it took three adults to hold me down. This was his first real memory in life. There we were, standing in the office of the Methodist Orphans' Home in Jackson, and our mother and oldest brother were about to drive away and leave us behind. The only person I knew there was John; everyone else had disappeared. I was three years and eight months old.

The fight went on for about an hour. I used some very bad words, and the matron took me to the bathroom and washed my mouth out with soap. She was a very plain-looking lady, with short hair and bangs, just like most ladies back then wore their hair, and no makeup. She had on a typical dress for the time, the kind that looked like it'd been made out of flour sacks. Flour sacks came with little flowers printed on them because everybody made clothing out of them when the flour was all used up. They were pretty and colorful prints, but everybody still knew they were flour sack dresses.

Dub explained to me in later years that all these arrangements had been made in advance. The sheriff had contacted some church people over in Jackson to arrange for all three of us boys to be put in the orphanage. But Dub found out about it, and convinced my mother that he could help her with the new baby that was coming if she'd keep him with her. That was why he'd been seated on the other side of her, and why he hadn't gone in with us when that girl had tricked us into going inside. It was the darkest moment in my young life, and I still have trouble thinking about it.

🌲

Chapter 3
Where's My Momma?

The Methodist Orphans' Home was as good as it could be, considering the number of kids there. There were not enough adults to run the place, so each matron had charge of a large number of children. There was plenty of food and clothing, and they did the best they could do.

Most of the children there were either true orphans, or they came from unwed mothers. Few, if any, were ever adopted by anyone. Most lived their entire childhood in the home. All the children were disturbed because their mothers had left them, and they were too young to understand. The matrons didn't want to get too close to the kids and bond with them, so they kept their distance. As a result, you had a home full of children who were starved for love and affection.

In my mind, I thought my mother would show up some day and everything would be just fine. That thought never left me. The same thought was on the mind of every child in the home.

I was put in a dormitory for the three- to five-year-olds. Girls and boys were kept in separate dorms. One of the girls from ages twelve to sixteen gave me a bath, put a pair of pajamas on me and tried to get me to sleep. They would do this for us every night.

Once we were all in bed and the lights were out, I would hear the saddest sound I have ever heard. All the kids began to cry and call out for their mothers before they went to sleep – and I was the loudest one in the pack. We finally drifted off to sleep, with tears still wet on our faces and pillows.

The next morning, we got up and the teenage girls dressed each of us, lined us up and took us to breakfast. This was new for me, so I didn't fight or start any trouble. They lined us around the table, with the matron seated at the head of it. She was just as plain as the woman the day before, only this one had her hair pulled back in a bun. After we had all gotten to our seats, she said, "Silence!"

Waiting for silence to ensue, she finally said, "Joe will now say the blessing. Please, Joe, say the blessing for the food."

I looked around and did not say a word. What was she talking about?

She said, "Joe, here at the home, we thank God for our food and we are askin' you to thank God for our food."

Again, I took my time, looking all around the table set with dishes and food, and the other kids sitting around it. They were all looking at me, waiting. After a minute or so, I shouted to the matron, "You ain't my mother!"

I jumped on the table and kicked everything off it. Food, plates, napkins, glasses. The shattering dishes and glasses made a terrible racket. Children were screaming, running and hiding. I yelled at the matron, "*You* say the blessin'. Not me. *You* say the blessin'!"

Finally, the matron got me off the table. Some old lady hogtied me and locked me in a closet until I could calm down. When they got me out of the closet, they again washed my mouth out with soap. Breakfast was over.

One of the teenage girls who lived in the home calmed me down. I seemed to respond more to her than to the matrons. She brought me some food afterward, so I wouldn't completely miss out on breakfast.

As time went by, I fell in line with the daily routine at the home. But it always seemed like I was being punished for something. I never liked or trusted the adults. Nobody ever touched or hugged us; we were just like sticks of wood to them. They didn't mistreat us, just never showed us any love.

Most of the three-, four- and five-year-olds played in a small area assigned to us. It was under a big oak tree on the grounds of the home. The other boys my age and I played there and we were not allowed to leave that place. They dressed us all in shorts and shirts for play time. I made friends with a little black-haired boy named David Poe.

One day, not long after I'd arrived, we were playing under the oak tree and I saw a man way across the grounds. All the matrons were women, and it was unusual to see a man. "Who's that?" I asked David.

"Who?"

"That man, over there, with them older boys followin' him. Who is that?" He was passing within about two hundred feet of our play area. The group following him consisted of boys from about seven to ten years old. He was leading a little Shetland pony, and the boys were taking turns riding on it.

"Oh. That's Mister MacDonald. He's the superintendent of the home."

"We gon' get to ride that pony next?" I asked.

"Oh, no, we're too young," said David.

"Well, why not?"

David acted like everybody knew that, and said, "'cause, silly, we *too young*. We'd fall off an' get hurt. When we get older, we can ride just like they doin'."

Mr. McDonald looked like the kind of guy I could admire, and would love to spend time with. And, yet, I was scared to death of him. He always seemed to spend his time with the older boys, never with us.

The older boys also disappeared on Sunday mornings. "Where are they going?" I asked David.

"To Sunday School," he said.

"What's Sunday School?"

"That's where they teach you all about God and such."

"Why don't we go?"

"We're too young. We'll get to go when we're older."

David and I would become best friends during my time in the home. Many years later, when I went back to a reunion of children who'd lived there, I asked someone about him. They remembered him, but nobody knew what had ever become of my friend.

The matron who watched over us kept her distance from us, and never talked to us except to discipline any children who did not behave. She usually read a book. We were all dying for love, but the matrons didn't want us to bond with them because of the possibility of heartaches down the road if any of the children ever left the home.

On several occasions, I wandered off, going to look for my mother. It was not very hard to get away, because the matron really wasn't paying close attention to what we were doing. They always found me within a short time, and brought me back. I was never able to get very far.

Not long after the weather got cold, there was a lot of work going on around the home. They were putting up green holly branches, with their red berries, and even a fresh cedar tree. The smell filled the air. The older children helped make ornaments for the Christmas tree out of tinfoil. We had a big dinner, then they gathered all of us together around the tree to sing Christmas carols. I didn't know the songs, but I was a good singer, and could fake my way through them pretty well.

The matron said, "Santa will bring you goodies if you are all good children." They hung a stocking at the foot of each of our beds, and filled it with candy and fruits. Not all the children were there for these festivities. "Where did they go?" I asked David.

"Some families from the churches come by and get some of us to take home with them for Christmas, then bring us back here after it's over."

"Well, if they can take you home for Christmas, why can't you stay there all the time?"

"Joe Abb, you ask a lot of questions! I don't know. That's just the way it is."

One day, the matron said to us, "Today, we have a special treat for you children! We're going to show y'all a picture show. Does anybody know what a picture show is?"

None of us raised our hands or said anything, because we were all too young to have remembered seeing picture shows before. We were also a little suspicious, because she was much perkier than usual.

"Well, I'm sure y'all are going to enjoy it. You must remember to sit still during the picture show and don't talk to your neighbors while it's playing. Now, line up so we can go over to the thee-ay-ter."

Even though we didn't know what a picture show was, we lined up like we were told. I was not too happy about missing our morning play time outside, but if this was something special, I certainly didn't want to miss out on it. I wasn't too happy about having to sit still, either, but maybe it wouldn't take too long.

When we got to the theater, they wanted us to sit in chairs that had been set up in rows, all facing a big, white screen in the front of the room. Other children from the different age groups were there, too. I looked for Brother John, but couldn't sit with him because we were made to sit with our own age groups. Another of the matrons went up front and said, "Quiet, please, children..." She waited a minute for silence before continuing, "Today's picture show stars the delightful Miss Shirley Temple. I'm sure you'll all enjoy it. Now, please remember to be quiet and sit still during the picture show!"

They turned out the lights in the room, and started showing moving pictures on the screen in front of us. All the pictures were in black and white, like photographs, but they were moving like in real life. The picture show had music and dancing, and it was not exactly my cup of tea. It was interesting for a few minutes, because of the novelty of it, but I was getting fidgety within a very short time. By the time it was over, I didn't care if I ever saw a picture show again. We were marched over to the dining room for lunch afterward. I couldn't wait to get outside and play with my friends.

They showed us picture shows several times after this. I remember seeing *Snow White and the Seven Dwarves*, but it didn't make much sense to me. I never could understand those little people. Some of the picture shows we saw featured Spanky McFarland, and others were about cowboys and Indians, which I really liked. That was much better to me than all that singing and dancing. I'd never heard about cowboys and Indians before, and those picture shows really made me want to be a cowboy. Cowboys got to ride horses, and I kept thinking about riding that Shetland pony like the older boys did. When we played under the oak tree after seeing those picture shows, we always played cowboys and Indians.

Even though I slept in the same dormitory as my brother, John, I didn't get to talk to him very often. He was eighteen months older than me, and in a different age group at the home. The matrons tried to keep me away from him because they thought seeing him made me more defiant. In reality, it was comforting to have him near, but that was about to change.

John's age group somehow all got the itch. This was a disease kids used to get that would make them itch all over. Even though the home was very clean, the boys John's age took their own baths, and some of them probably didn't keep as clean as those of us who were bathed by the teenage girls. They stripped down all the boys in John's group, and covered them from head to toe with a mixture of lard and sulfur. The sulfur made them all smell like rotten eggs. To keep the smell out of the beds, they made the boys sleep on quilts laid on the floor until the itch went away. They also transferred them to another building, and that was the last time I'd see my brother for many years.

From where I stayed, I could see the single-story white building where they had taken John to live. It was about 300 feet away from our building, and slightly downhill from us. Every time I'd see anyone coming or going from that building, I'd look for John, but never could see him. The people running the home thought this would help them control me, to keep me away from my brother, but it just made me more determined to get out of there and find my momma.

Chapter 4
The Road Out

At the time I was there, the Methodist Orphans' Home was so large it had its own school. Eventually, the day came when my age group was ready to start the first grade. When they tried to let me start school, I got destructive again, and it was back to the closet for me. They decided that I was not quite six years old, since my birthday wasn't until October, so they would not let me go to class any more. I continued to play under the oak tree with David and the other five-year-olds.

Most days, I'd see the group of older boys, following Mr. McDonald and heading down a dirt road behind the orphanage. The road was about eight feet wide. On either side of it grew tall, green plants of some sort. I couldn't see where the boys in Mr. McDonald's group were going, and this bothered me. They would disappear over the hill, laughing and singing together. Before sunset, I'd see Mr. McDonald leading them back from down that wonderful, mysterious, garden-like road.

Sometimes I would go to sleep at night dreaming of what was at the end of that beautiful road. The strains of *Oh, Susannah* and *Workin' on the Railroad* would run through my head as I imagined myself going with the group of older boys down the dirt road. We were all singing together in the same key, just like I'd heard them singing every day, and we sounded really good.

One day, before he'd gotten moved away from me, I was able to see brother John when we were on the way out to play, and told him all about the road.

"After you turn twelve, you can go down that road," he told me.

"How do you know that?"

"One of them other boys told me. You okay, Joe Abb?"

"John, when we gonna get out of here and go back to Momma?"

"I don't know, Joe Abb. Just try to be good, and do what the matrons tell you to do."

Suddenly, a matron appeared, and John was whisked away from me as quickly as I had found him. I never did get to ask him what went on down that road.

Alas, in my time at the orphanage, I never did get to travel down the dirt road, with its lush green fields on either side. Later in life, I would find out that it led to a 36-acre farm that raised all the food we ate at the home. Mr. McDonald had started the farm, and put the teenage boys to work at it. The rows of tall, green plants I saw were corn. They also grew peas, beans, potatoes, tomatoes and lots more. The Shetland pony was even kept at the farm.

In addition to their work with us smaller children, the teenage girls in the home did all the cooking and washing of clothes. There was a little brick building that was the washhouse, and they'd spend hours there with a scrub board and a pan, washing all the clothes and bed linens for the home. It was something I always took for granted while I was there; there were always clean clothes to wear, fresh sheets on the beds and good food on the table. I never even thought about where it came from, or who did the work to put it there. It was only many years later, at a reunion, that one of the girls told me about this.

With John not around, I continued to give them problems at the home, pitching fits and throwing tantrums whenever something didn't go the way I wanted. One afternoon, I walked down the hill from under the old oak tree again, and I got farther this time.

The city of Jackson was about twenty blocks away from the home. After leaving, I made my way there, not knowing where I was going, but just wanting to get away and get back to my momma. It was getting dark, and I was walking around in the edges of Jackson, watching all the street lights come on. It was fascinating! I'd never been in a real city like this before.

A man came up to me and I heard his deep voice asking, "Boy, where is your mother?" I looked up to see a tall, fit and handsome man in a uniform, complete with a hat, badge and gun. He seemed like he could be a father.

"I don't know," I said. "I have been looking for her for a long, long time, but I don't know where she is. I'd like to find her, but I don't know where she is."

"Well, you come with me, and we'll find your mother," said the policeman. Boy, I thought he must be a good guy, if he could find my mother. He was the best guy in the world!

He took me by the hand and we walked through town together, ending up at the police station. He gave me some bubble gum to keep me busy – he must have had children of his own to understand that boys my age needed something to keep them busy – and I thought I had found a friend for life.

At the station, I sat in the policeman's lap and was questioned by several officers. "When did you see your mother last?" one said.

12

"I don't know. I don't know when I saw her. It's been a long, long time ago since I've seen my mother."

"Well, then, where is your father?" another said.

"I don't know." It was true; I may have had some vague memory of my father being sent to prison, but I didn't know where that was.

"Do you have a brother?"

"Yessuh, but they took him away to this big, white house, and I have not seen him lately."

By this time, they were beginning to suspect where I had come from. "Let me just make a quick phone call," said one of the officers.

He went over to the phone while the other policemen continued to play games with me. They were all very nice, and I felt right at home with them. When he came back, the policeman said, "Yes, they're missing a five-year-old boy, and this one fits the description."

I was still playing with my new friends when the car arrived from the orphans' home to take me back. A man and a woman walked in. I didn't know them, but something told me they were from the home. Of course, I was disappointed when they came in to get me. "But these people's gonna help me find my momma," I protested.

"You really want to go back to your mother, don't you, Joe?" asked the official from the home.

"Yes, I do," I said. "I was tryin' to find her, and now these p'licemen say they gon' help me."

"Okay, Joe, let's go on back to the home tonight, and we'll help you find her tomorrow."

"You promise?"

"Yes, we will."

For the first time, when they took me back to the home, they didn't punish me for running away. They took me in and gave me some leftovers for dinner, then one of the teenage girls bathed me, put some pajamas on me and put me to bed.

Chapter 5
Going Home

The next morning, after breakfast, I returned to the dormitory to find what few possessions I had packed and ready to go. It was time for the matron to take the five-year-olds outside to play, but she told me, "Joe, you're not goin' outside with us today."

"Why not?" I figured this was going to be my punishment for running away. They'd never packed up my things before, though.

"You'll see. Here's Darlene now to get you ready."

The other kids lined up to follow the matron outside to play, but they were all looking back at me when they left. It was the last time I would ever see them.

Darlene was one of the teenage girls who'd bathed and dressed us before. She came in and said, "Okay, Joe Abb, this little suit and tie should be just the perfect fit for you."

"Why you dressin' me up, just so they can punish me?" I asked.

"Oh," she laughed, "You ain't bein' punished. They said somethin' about you goin' on a trip. Here, now, put on this clean shirt."

I could only imagine what kind of closets they'd found to put me in, that I had to take a trip to get to them. Putting on the shirt and pants, I wondered just where they were taking me.

"Now, let's tie your tie. You know how to tie a tie?"

"Naw." I'd never worn a tie before in my life, but I seemed to remember seeing a few grown men wearing them, like that nice policeman in Jackson.

"Well, I'll get it on you..." She twisted the necktie into a knot at my neck. "There. Now for the jacket...put your arms in here..." as she pulled the jacket onto me and straightened it. "Put on your socks...and your shoes...here, I'll tie 'em for you..."

"I know how to tie my shoes!"

"Okay, then, you do it...There, now, you look just like a little man! Follow me, and we gon' get you started on your trip."

I picked up the bundle of clothes they'd packed for me and followed her down to the office.

"Ah, Darlene, you've brought him. Good," said the secretary. "I'll tell Mister MacDonald." She disappeared into the office behind her desk, and I could hear the grownups talking in there.

"Where am I goin'?" I asked Darlene.

"I don't know."

"Will John be comin' with me?"

"Who?"

"My brother, John. He got moved over to that little white building when them boys in his group got the itch. I sure would love to see John again."

"Oh. I don't know, but I'm sure you gon' be fine from here on. Take care, Joe Abb." She actually hugged me, which nobody ever did there.

I sat there outside Mr. McDonald's office, waiting on somebody to tell me what was going on, half expecting to see John walking into the office, but not really knowing if I should have that much hope.

Finally, the secretary emerged from the office. "Okay, Joe Abb, we gon' take you down to the Trailways station and put you on a bus. You gon' be travelin' alone, but the driver will look after you."

"Where'm I goin'?"

"To Ackerman. Can you remember that?"

"Yes'm." I'd heard of Ackerman before. That's where my father had been taken when the sheriff arrested him. I remembered Dub telling me about it. Was I being arrested, like Dad was?

They put me in the back seat of a car, still hanging onto my bundle of clothes, and drove me into Jackson to the Trailways bus station. The man drove, and a woman was with him to take care of me. We went inside to a tall counter with a little cage on top of it and a man standing behind an opening in the cage. They bought my ticket there, then we went outside to where the bus was waiting. It smelled of diesel fumes.

A man in a uniform was standing by the door of the bus, taking people's tickets as they boarded. He was a young, handsome guy with dark hair that started way up high on his forehead. They waited until all the other people had gotten on the bus, then took me up to him and said, "This is Joe Abb Overby. He's travelin' by himself to Ackerman, and will be met by a woman there named Candace Overby. Will you watch over him on the trip?"

"Sure, I will," said the driver, then he bent down to my level. "You ready to go, li'l man?"

"Yessuh," I said.

"You ever ridden on a bus before, boy?"

"Naw, suh."

"Well, we gon' have us a goooood trip over to Ackerman." He turned back to the adults. "He'll be fine. We do this all the time. I'll take good care of him."

"Thank you," said the lady from the home. "Now, Joe Abb, you mind the driver when he tells you to do somethin', you hear?"

"Yes'm."

The driver took me aboard the bus and put me in the seat right behind his. "Here you go, Joe – hey I made me a rhyme! How 'bout that? You just set right up here, an' watch all that purty scenery go by, and we'll get us on down the road."

I climbed into the seat. The driver took my bundle of clothes from me and put it in a little storage area up by the ceiling of the bus, above my seat. "This can go right up here. I'll get it down for you when we get there."

"Okay. We really goin' to see my momma?"

"Yessiree, sho' nuff sounds like we are. You been off visitin' with your relatives?" he asked as he climbed into the driver's seat. He pulled a lever and shut the doors to the bus.

"Nawsuh. So my brother ain't comin' with me?"

"I dunno. Your brother been visitin' them relatives with you?"

"Nawsuh, not really."

"Well, then why would he be comin' with you?"

"I dunno." It was too complicated to explain to him, and I wasn't sure I understood all of what was going on, either. The important thing was, I was going to see my momma!

The driver continued his conversation with me along the way, in between stops. That bus sure did stop a lot. Every little country town had people who needed to get on or off. I sat there and watched the trees going by so fast in between towns. I'd never seen anything like it before.

Late in the afternoon, we pulled into a little sawmill town with no paved streets, only gravel roads. Log trucks were all over the place. There were lots of wagons being pulled by mules. All the people seemed to be wearing bib overalls and straw hats. The driver picked up the microphone for the loudspeaker on the bus and said, "Ackerman." Then he stopped the bus at the station.

"What a great place to live!" I thought. The door opened. Nobody else was getting off there, just me. The driver turned to me and said, "Okay, li'l man, we here! Let me get that package for you." He reached up into the overhead bin and got my little bundle of clothes.

I bounded down the steps to the bus and saw a woman and man standing there. The driver came out right behind me and said, "Here's your momma, boy."

I looked at the woman standing there. She was very tiny, with reddish hair cut at about the nape of her neck. Her blue eyes looked out blankly from her freckled face. She was wearing a flowered skirt and blouse, one of those made from a flour sack. My slight memory of my mother made

16

me half recognize her. I ran over to her, wrapping my arms around her waist. Grabbing her with both arms, I hung on with everything I had.

Momma didn't say anything, and she didn't hug me back. Then, after a couple of minutes, I felt her cold hands pulling me loose from her. The man standing beside her was older, and I didn't know him. He was wearing an old, black felt hat. He had short black hair and was clean-shaven. He was a full-fleshed man, but not really heavy-set, dressed in regular pants and a shirt, not the bib overalls that most everybody else in the town was wearing. The man was my grandfather, my momma's father.

The bus driver kind of looked at us all a little funny, then said, "Well, folks, I'm glad he got here safe an' sound. I got a schedule to meet, so I'm fixin' to be on my way. Joe, you take care now, and be good for your momma!"

"Yessuh," I said.

The driver climbed back into his seat, closed the doors to the bus, and pulled away, leaving me standing there with Momma and Grandpa.

"Follow us, boy, we goin' home," said Grandpa. Momma still hadn't said a word.

"Yessuh," I said, and fell in behind them.

We walked forever and ever down a gravel road, then turned left onto a dirt road that turned into a small trail as we walked farther and farther back into the woods. I was so happy looking through the beautiful green trees along this former wagon road.

There was something lying in the road I'd never seen before. It looked sort of like a lemon. "Grampaw, what's that?" I asked.

"Them's maypops," he said.

"Maypops?"

"Yep. Grows on a vine along the ground. That 'un's ripe, there, but when they's green, you can stomp on 'em an' they'll pop real loud."

"Really?"

"Yep. Here's one now." He threw the green maypop on the ground and stomped on it, and it let out a loud, popping sound. I was thrilled with this new discovery, and insisted stomping on every maypop we saw along the roadway.

After a while, we got out of maypop country, and walked along in silence. Suddenly, my grandfather let out a big, loud fart. I looked around at him, and he said, "Was that you, boy, or did you step on one of them maypops?" I laughed and laughed.

My mother was embarrassed, and said, "Y'all boys stop that nasty talkin' right now! I don't wanna hear it no more." It was the first time she'd spoken since I'd arrived.

About two hours after leaving Ackerman, we arrived at our house.

Actually, it was a shack, where my mother and grandfather had been living. He had a good job with the WPA, which the locals had decided stood for "We Piddle Around." Grandpa was getting paid $1 a day, which was good money then. My mother just stayed around the house, cooking and washing for him. I have vague memories of my little sister, Lolly, being around at the shack. She'd been born while I was living in the home. Sometimes, Lolly would stay with some of my momma's cousins, but other times, she was with us.

The shack was so far out in the woods, and was the most beautiful house I'd ever seen. Not the shack itself, but all the green trees around it. Living in that large dorm at the home, being protected from the weather, I'd never been so close to nature. We were only let outside for short periods of time, and I couldn't believe I was going to be living in such a beautiful, natural place.

As we got up to the shack, I could hear cackling, and said, "What's that?"

"Them's chickens, boy," said Grandpaw. "Got 'em everywhere."

I could see several of them scratching around in the yard. When I ran over to the plump, fluffy birds, they ran away from me. They sure did stink!

Inside the shack were two rooms, one in front for cooking, and one in back, where we would sleep. There were windows in the outside walls that were always open, but they didn't have any screens, so the bugs could come right in. The wood floor had big cracks in it. Despite the chicken smell outside, the house seemed to be very clean on the inside.

The kitchen had a wood-burning cook stove, where my momma cooked. The dining table was made from sawmill-cut wood. There was a bench built into the wall, and the table was pushed up to it. There were a couple of cane-bottom chairs sitting on the outside of the table.

In the bedroom, there were two big, wooden beds with metal slats. The mattresses on them were stuffed with straw, because it was summer. There were some filthy sheets, then quilts on top of the mattresses.

When we got to the shack, nobody else was there. I explored inside, then made my way out to the front yard and the dirt trail that ran in front of the shack. As I was standing there, Dub came walking down the road, carrying his lunch pail and school books. He recognized me and yelled, "Joe Abb!"

I ran to Dub and we hugged. The lunch pail he was carrying was really an old lard bucket. Those used to be painted pretty with flowers so people could use them for other things once the lard was all gone, and they were using this one for Dub's lunch bucket. "You hungry, Joe Abb?" he said.

"Yeah, Dub. I ain't eat nothin' since breakfast."

"Ain't eat *any*thing."

"Huh?"

"It's 'I ain't eat *any*thing since breakfast.' You got to learn to use proper grammar, Joe Abb. Can't have no double negatives."

"Oh." I had no idea what he was talking about.

He opened his lunch pail and pulled out a cracker with peanut butter on it to give me. It didn't take me long to finish it, then we walked back to the shack together.

"So, did you learn that grammar stuff in school, Dub?" I asked.

"Yeah. They teach you lots of stuff there."

"What's school like? Is it fun? What do you do there?"

"Whoa, slow down, there Joe Abb. I'll tell you all about it. I reckon it's okay. We read and learn things and stuff. All about history, and geography and arithmetic, and all."

"Wow. I can't wait until I can go to school, too."

"You will, someday. You almost old enough now."

We got back to the shack and Momma said, "You boys wash yo' hands for supper."

"Okay, Momma," said Dub.

"Where's the bathroom?" I said.

"C'mon, Joe Abb, I'll show you where we wash up out here."

He took me outside on the porch to a bucket of water. The shack didn't have an indoor bathroom, nor did it have electricity or running water. We dipped a cup into the bucket, poured it over our hands, rubbed them around a little and dried them off on our pants.

"Where do we get our bath?" I asked my big brother.

"Bath? We don't take no bath. Sometimes go swimmin', but we don't take no baths." I was thrilled. No bath before bedtime! I was in hog heaven. Dub and I went back inside for supper.

"You boys set on that bench," said Grandpa.

We climbed in behind the table. Dub and I were eating out of a big, oval sardine can, but the adults had regular plates. They were sitting on the cane-bottomed chairs across the table from us.

"Can I get me a dish like Dub's?" I asked.

"Like Dub's?" said Momma.

"I want me a dish like Dub's."

"Well, sure, boy. We'll git you one just like it!" said Grandpa. "Now, dig in."

Dinner consisted of cornbread and milk. "No fish tonight," said Grandpa, "We done had to spend the day in Ackerman, gettin' you, boy. Gon' hafta learn you to fish."

That sounded great to me! "Grampaw?" I said.

"What, boy?"

"Ain't we gon' say grace?"

"Grace?"

"We always said grace in the home before we eat, y'know, to thank God for the food? You *must* say grace."

"By God, you right, son. Just bow your head and close them eyes, and then we'll start grace, just like they do in the home."

I closed my eyes and bowed my head, just like they'd taught me to do.

"Yer eyes closed, boy?"

"Yessuh, Grandaddy!"

"Okay, here we go," he said. "Touch the lips, past the gums, look out asshole, here it comes! Now, you go on and eat all you want, boy." Even Dub was giggling now.

I thought my grandaddy must be the greatest person in the world.

Chapter 6
The End of the Rainbow

It didn't take me long to get used to life at the shack. Grandpa and I slept together, and Dub slept in the other bed with our momma. Dub showed me where we got our water, which was at a spring across the trail from the shack. You had to walk down some steps about a hundred feet, then there it was. The woods were beautiful, with little streams and waterfalls all over the place running down to the Choctaw Creek below us.

My grandfather was different from the only man I ever remembered being around, Mr. McDonald, back at the home. Grandpa cussed, chewed tobacco, stole, and lied. What's more, I was free to do as many of those things as I wanted. Deep in my heart, I knew they weren't right, but the freedom was intoxicating, and I had to try everything at least once. Dub would keep me in line, though, and would say, "Don't act out like Grampaw, Joe Abb."

"Why not?"

"Because, the devil will get you!" That was his standard answer for whenever I was doing something he didn't think was right. "The devil will get you." My momma was more direct: "You jus' like yo' daddy!" she'd say.

A couple days after I arrived at the shack, it started to rain in the morning and continued all day. We had to put pots all over the floor to catch drips from the leaks in our roof. I thought all of this was the greatest thing I'd ever seen. At the home, we'd always been kept inside when it rained. Grandpa wouldn't let me go outside while it was raining, either, but as soon as it stopped, I ran out into the woods. Everything smelled so fresh and new, and it was like nothing I'd ever experienced before. The beautiful, green trees were even more brilliant after the rain.

In addition to the fish we'd catch in the Choctaw Creek, we'd eat things like chicken, or maybe rabbits or squirrels that Grandpa had shot in the woods. But his favorite meat, by far, was possum. There were also vegetables from a garden we had down the trail from the shack, and eggs, courtesy of the chickens, for breakfast.

He may not have been too honest, but my granddaddy knew all kinds

21

of ways to survive. He used to trade bulldog pups at the swap meet in Ackerman. I don't know where he got them. One day, he brought home a litter of bulldog pups. I was thrilled, and had a wonderful time playing with them.

"Boy, bring them dogs over here," said Grandpa. He was sitting next to an old tree stump, holding an axe.

"Why, Grandaddy, what you gon' do with 'em?" I suddenly became afraid for my new little friends.

"Jus' gettin' 'em ready to sell. Now, you cain't keep them dogs as pets. They's to be sold in town. Now, you jus' hold that'n still here on this stump."

I did as he told me. He pulled the little dog's tail out and quickly chopped it off with the axe. The dog started whimpering from the pain, and I began to cry.

"Granddaddy, don't hurt 'im like that!" I wailed.

"Now, boy, them dogs can't feel no pain. They's jus' dogs, anyways." He took some coal oil—that was what we called kerosene—and started painting it on the puppy's wounded stub of a tail. The little dog was whimpering so, I knew he could feel the pain.

"Whatcha doin' that for, Granddaddy?"

"That keeps the flies from gettin' on his tail an' givin' him worms." He looked at my tear-stained face and said, "You jus' too tender-hearted, boy. Now, catch that next 'un and put 'im up here."

Regretfully, I helped my grandfather dock the remaining dogs' tails.

Grandpa taught me all the names of the different types of chickens we had. There were Rhode Island Reds, Domenicks, white-legged chickens, and the small Banty chickens. We fed them with corn bought from the local farmers. Dub would come home from school and feed the chickens in the afternoons, and he let me help him. There were chicken hawks in the area, and whenever we'd hear the chickens start cackling, we'd know a hawk was swooping down to get one. They'd go into the brush to hide until it was safe to come back out. With all the trees around the shack, it was hard for a hawk to catch and kill a chicken. There was too much tree coverage.

One afternoon, I kept hearing chickens cackling, but couldn't understand why, since I couldn't see a hawk anywhere. I walked out behind the shack and into the woods, getting ever closer to the cackling. Lord have mercy, I found a hen's nest out in the woods! There must have been fifteen or twenty eggs in it. I went screaming to my mother, "Momma, come see what I found!"

Momma was sitting in the front yard in a cane-bottomed chair. I was so excited and happy that I had found all these eggs, and thought she would be so proud of me for finding this big prize. She seemed to be happy, and followed me to the hen's nest. We gathered the eggs and took them back to the house, but she never did tell me she was proud of me. Momma wasn't the type to say too much.

Grandpa was at work during the day, working for the WPA. Dub was in school. He'd leave every morning, walking down the old wagon road, to where the school bus came by on the gravel road to pick him up. I'd wait for him to come walking back in the afternoons, running down to meet him, and we'd walk the last part together.

Dub had missed a lot of school from all the moving around we'd done when my dad had been sent to prison, so he was a little behind. Momma's family didn't value education; neither she nor my grandfather could read. But Dub was smart. He was my rock. For some reason, I felt safe when he was with me, more so than with my mother or grandfather.

During the days, my mother never had much to do with me, so I'd wander off into the beautiful woods. There was a boy about my age who lived down the trail with the Maynard family, and sometimes we'd play together. The garden patch was right down there, and we were playing there one day when the Maynard boy pulled these long, orange roots out of the ground.

"What's that?" I asked him.

"These? Why, them's carrots, silly," he said. "You ain't never seen no carrots before?"

Well, of course I'd seen carrots when we'd eaten them in the home, but I had no idea they came out of the ground. "Yeah, but not like them," I said.

"Well, they's carrots. Here, rinse one off an' taste it," and he passed one over to me.

The color was beautiful, so brilliant and orange, as I poured a dipper of water over it. I bit into the wet carrot and was just amazed. I had to show Dub when he got home from school that day.

"Dub, you seen them carrots down the road?"

"*Those* carrots. Yeah, sure, Joe Abb." I couldn't believe he could be so casual about such a miracle – what did grammar matter when we had carrots?!

One day around noon, a big, red truck pulled up in the yard. It barely made it down that old wagon trail running up to the shack. I ran right out in the front yard to see that red pickup truck. It was probably a county truck that was working on the WPA project. A smallish, countrified-looking man got out of the truck. He was nice-looking and friendly, and appeared to be a little bit older than my mother. The small, thin stranger had on khaki pants, a white shirt and clodhopping shoes. His hair was neatly combed, and he was clean-shaven.

My mother came out of the house into the front yard from the porch when the truck pulled up. True to her nature, she just looked at him and didn't say a word. She looked especially nice today, like she'd cleaned herself up a little.

"Hey, Cannie," the driver of the truck finally said.

"Hey, Ben. How you?"

"Awright, I reckon. You?"

She just nodded.

I was fascinated by this red truck, and couldn't take my eyes off it. Ben and my mother went up on the front porch to sit in the cane-bottomed chairs. They started talking and laughing together. I wanted to be included in the conversation, but had a feeling they didn't want me around.

"You goin' out in the woods today, Joe Abb?" she asked me.

"Naw, I don't think so," I said.

My mother would say to Ben from time to time, "Let's don't do nothin' now, while he's here."

Finally, the driver said to me, "Young man, you wanna play with this truck?"

My eyes lit up. "I sure do!"

"Well, I'm gon' let you get inside my truck for 'bout, oh, maybe twenty, thirty minutes, and I'm gon' lock them doors so nobody can get in there with you. That way, it's gon' be all yours. Then, I'll come out an' get you."

Boy, this was the kind of man I really liked! I got in the truck, he locked me in the cab, and my mother and he went into the house. I sat there and played like I was driving, turning the wheel and playing at shifting the gears. My feet couldn't reach the pedals, and I didn't have the keys, so there was really no harm I could do.

I was starting to get bored when Ben finally came back out of the house to get me. Momma came out on the porch and said, "Bye." She always was a woman of few words. Ben said to me, "I'll be back and let you drive my truck again. Would you like that?"

"I sure would like to drive this truck again! Come back anytime. Come back tomorrow! I would like to drive your truck again and again!" Ben was a frequent caller, as I recall.

The weather started to change. It began to rain a lot. The old shack had a tin roof, and at night I'd go to bed and fall asleep listening to the rain falling on that tin roof. I could sleep all night listening to the rainfall. Next morning, I'd get up and go outside to use the bathroom.

When the rain would stop for a short time, I'd go outside and play in the woods. There were even more waterfalls after all the rain, and it was amazing. The land there was hilly, just enough so there were small waterfalls coming from every direction. This was like heaven for me. I thought I could live here forever and be the happiest boy in the world.

Some nights, we'd sit around the fireplace and cook on the fire. Most every night, my grandfather taught me to cook. I'd never seen anybody cook before. One of my favorite things to do was to cook sweet potatoes in the fireplace. He'd dig a hole in the hot ashes, bury the sweet potatoes, then put the hot coals on top of them. In about an hour, those potatoes would be cooked. The big, black pots were always hanging over the fire with something cooking – soup, stew, or even Granddaddy's possum. Whenever I got hungry, I'd eat whatever was in the pot.

Momma would fry cornbread in a big, black skillet. I really liked that fried cornbread. She used plenty of lard in the skillet to keep the cornbread from sticking to the pan.

My grandfather loved to eat mush. I'd never heard of mush before; we never ate it at the home. It was sort of like grits, but cooked a little different. That made it come out a lot thicker than grits.

One afternoon, I walked out behind the shack and down a slope about six hundred feet away. The woods were very thick in that area, with lots of brush, and everything was so very green. The deeper I went into the woods, the greener it would get. Even the tree types would change. I was fascinated by this, and kept going deeper into the woods.

There were cedar trees, so very green and straight, with beautiful limbs. Ahead were several holly trees with red berries. I remembered these from Christmas time in the orphan's home. I thought I had arrived at the end of the rainbow. I knew I would never leave this place, with the beautiful green Christmas trees with thousands of red berries hanging from them. Little did I know I was descending into the bottomlands of the Choctaw Creek.

The creek was only about three hundred feet from where I was standing. I sat down on a tree log for almost half an hour. Things got very, very quiet. I kept looking up into the trees.

Suddenly, I saw the prettiest thing in the world jumping from limb to limb. It looked like a fireball of red fur. It was a beautiful red fox squirrel. I sat there, unmoving, as he jumped and danced through the trees, until he disappeared. What more could a six-year-old boy want?

There were also many birds in the woods. The quieter I was, the closer they all came to me. There were two red-headed woodpeckers that got so close I could have reached out and touched them with a rock, but I didn't. I didn't want to hurt them. I wanted to come back and watch them all again.

After a while, I started to wonder which way I'd come into this place. I knew the creek was close by, but I couldn't see it. I sat there a while, alone, then began to get afraid.

Suddenly, out of nowhere, I heard brother Dub calling, "Joe Abb! Joe Abb, it's time to come home!" I was so happy I started running toward the voice of my brother. It was not very far from the shack, and Dub had just gotten home from school.

That night, we all sat around the fireplace and ate whatever was in the black pots. It started to rain, and we went to bed shortly after eating. I fell asleep and dreamed of my wonder world in the woods all over again, with the beautiful red squirrels, woodpeckers, and many other colorful birds in the trees.

Chapter 7
Another Mouth to Feed

One Sunday morning, my grandfather took me on a long walk through the woods and showed me where he worked. There were large, wooden toolboxes full of tools – shovels, axes, rakes, picks, you name it – that were all locked up. They had big signs on the tool boxes that said, "FEDERAL EQUIPMENT – PENALTY BY LAW – DO NOT TAKE WITHOUT PERMISSION." This was the federal WPA project.

This particular project was to build a dam across the Choctaw Creek that would create a lake. The dam was almost completed, and the water was beginning to back up. By then, it was only about 400-600 feet from our shack.

As Grandpa and I walked home through the bushes, he found all kinds of tools in the woods. I thought he was the greatest and smartest person in the world, finding all those tools and equipment laying in the bushes! In reality, he had stolen them all, hiding them away while he was working, only to come back later, find them again and take them home. He'd file off the serial numbers and sell them at the flea market in Ackerman. He only had one more week of work, so he was stealing all he could at this point.

The water was getting higher and higher each day as the dam was being completed. I could now see it from the back door of our shack. A few days later, two men drove up in front of the house in a green pickup truck with some kind of insignia on the door. They said, "Young!" Young was my grandaddy's first name. "Getchyer sorry goddamn ass out here!"

Grandpa went out on the front porch.

"Dammit, Young, you told us y'all had done moved outta this place. What you doin' still here?"

He said, "Okay, Wilbur."

"This here's serious, Young. You know this place is about to be under water. Y'all got to get gone!"

"I'll be out, Wilbur. I'll be gone in 24 hours." I believe Wilbur and the other man not only knew my grandfather, they were actually related to him. They'd all been raised right there in Choctaw County.

I could not believe what I was hearing. My beautiful woods, all those lovely cedars and hollies, and all the colorful animals were being flooded

27

by the new Choctaw Lake.

We went to bed that night, hoping it would not rain and make the waters rise even faster. I went to sleep thinking of all the beautiful green trees, the hollies and their berries, the birds and squirrels being flooded out behind the shack, deep in the Choctaw bottomland.

When we got up the next morning, brother Dub went down the trail out of sight, as usual, to the gravel road to catch the school bus. Left at the shack were Grandpa and my mother. They were whispering to each other and looking at each other. I could hear little bits of the conversation.

"...know that project's over. Ain't no more work comin' this..."

"Well, what can we..."

I felt very afraid. "Momma, what y'all talkin' about?"

"Findin' us a place to live," she said.

They continued talking in low voices so that I could not understand anything, and looking at me as they were talking.

"You gon' put me back in the orphans' home?" I finally asked. It was my greatest fear.

"No, we would not do such a thing like that," said my mother.

"Please, please, don't put me back in that orphans' home. I wanna stay with you an' Grampaw."

She said, "Don't worry, Joe Abb. Let's all go for a walk and think of somethin' else."

That sounded like a great thing to do. We went walking through what was left of those beautiful woods, where Grandpa had "found" all those tools he'd stolen from the government. When we got to the WPA worksite, the big toolboxes, the dirt diggers and other big equipment were all gone. They had moved out of the area because the dam was now completed.

Where the toolboxes had been, there was a large bank overlooking the new Choctaw Lake, which was a beautiful body of water.

Grandpa said, "Boy, there's lots of fish in this here lake. Sometimes, you can jus' set here and watch 'em jump...Look out there–one jus' jumped!"

I had to see this for myself. I got to the edge of the very steep bank, where it dropped straight down, as close as I could possibly get without falling.

"Just keep on lookin'," said Grandpa. "You gon' see a big 'un jump straight up." He got real close to me and pulled me up close to the bank, as close as I could get.

Suddenly, he grabbed me by the shoulder. I looked for my mother. She was standing about fifteen feet away from us, and started crying.

"Please, don't let's do this to him. Don't let's do this to him. Let's all go home!" she shouted through her tears.

He finally let me go, and I ran over to my mother. None of us said anything as we walked back to the shack that was soon to be underwater.

It was many years before I could even recall this incident. When I was about 50 years old, I told Dub the whole story. "They were just going to tell people I'd wandered off, and had gotten drowned in the lake. I used to wander off all the time, and nobody would've thought anything more of it."

He said, "They were the type to do this." He went on to tell me that they'd tried several times to get rid of him, but he was older and craftier than I. He loved his mother more than anything, but although he was her first child, she never loved him any more than any of the rest of us. She was always trying to give us away, to get rid of us in any way she could.

The next morning, we packed up all our rags in a pickup truck, along with all our chickens in crates and three hound dogs. All I could see was the fast-rising Choctaw Lake. It had rained all night, but stopped while we loaded up and moved on. I'm not sure who owned the truck, but the driver was my mother's friend, Ben.

There was a galvanized washtub in the back of the truck, where our mother used to wash our clothes. It was sitting upside down, and that's where I sat for the trip over to the next house. Looking back as the old shack disappeared behind a curve in the road, I said, "Goodbye to my end of the rainbow."

Dub laughed and said, "Joe Abb, you just make those crazy things up."

"Where we goin', Dub?"

"Lawdy, mercy, Joe Abb, who knows?" he said as we bounced along the old wagon road in the back of that pickup truck with everything we owned.

Chapter 8
The Flatlands

Traveling on those old dirt roads in the back of a pickup truck was rough. I finally got off the galvanized washtub and sat on some toe sacks that were stacked in the back of the truck. That's what we called potato sacks, was "toe sacks." They were a lot easier on my rear-end than the washtub.

God only knows how many chickens there were in that truck, riding along with me and Dub. Between them cackling and crapping all over the back of the pickup, and the hound dogs barking, I didn't know whether to stay in the back of the truck or jump out and run alongside. They wouldn't have left me behind, since the truck was only going between five and eight miles an hour on that rough wagon road. It wasn't even really a road at all; it'd been used to haul logs for the sawmill years before.

It took us about two hours to arrive at our new shack. This one was owned by a family named McClure. It looked almost exactly like the one we'd just left, except that it was newer. There were no beautiful trees around this one, though, only tall pine trees around the house. Listening to the lonely winds blowing through the tops of those pine trees gave me the creeps and shivers.

"I don't like this place," I said to Dub. "Let's run away and go back. Can you remember the way back?"

"Naw, and you better not try and find your way back. You gon' get lost and the devil'll get you."

We were still standing in front of our new two-room shack. This house didn't even have an outdoor john, like our previous one had. Still no running water or electricity, either. Momma and Grandpa turned all those chickens loose.

When we went inside, we were surprised by what we found.

"Hey, look here, they's part of this floor in the front room, ain't even finished!" Only about two-thirds of the floor in the front room had been done, and you could see the dirt underneath the rest. The dogs and chickens had come inside from underneath the house, and were running all over the place.

"Well, this back room ain't got no floor at all! It's just all dirt."

"Joe Abb, Dub, y'all run them chickens an' dogs out of the house," said our mother.

Dub and I started chasing the livestock out of the house, only to find that the floor planks that had been put in place had not been nailed down. I stepped on one and fell down underneath the house. There I lay, with all those nasty chickens and dogs, below the floor of the house. We were all tangled together under there, everybody screaming and hollering, "Joe Abb, you hurt, son?"

I shouted back, "Just scared to death."

Once they got me out from under the floor, they nailed down some of the floor planking in the two corners of the living room, then set up the two beds there. Even with some of the planks nailed into place, the hound dogs still slept under my and Grandpa's bed that night. We hadn't found the water spring yet, so I had to sleep with all that chicken crap all over me. None of us ever bathed, anyway, so the smell wasn't all that noticeable. Dub and Momma slept together in the other bed. Sister Lolly was staying with Momma's cousins again.

Next morning, the biggest task ahead of us was to get all the floor planking nailed down. There was still a section in the front room that didn't have a floor at all. Before the floor work could be done, though, we had to find a water spring and get water to drink and clean up. This land was flat, and springs are hard to find in flat country. We all went out looking for one behind the house. Momma and brother Dub went to the left, while Grandpa and I went to the right. Those were the lower-lying lands, and there would most likely be water in those directions. Grandpa carried a shovel and an axe with us.

"Now, Joe Abb, if you want to find a spring, you keep looking for those big water bugs," said Grandpa. "You'll see 'em cluster up, and when you see that, there'll be water there. A lot of insects, and especially the water bugs, hang around where there's some water."

"Okay, Grampaw."

We kept going through the woods, and the ground was getting a little soggy. Finally, we noticed a cluster of water bugs swarming around. We headed directly toward them and found a small bank that dropped off into the swamp area. The ground was very damp and kind of mushy. Grandpa took the shovel and started digging out, cutting roots and everything. Finally, he hit a small vein of water coming out of the bank.

We went back to the house, where Momma and Dub were just getting back, also. "We couldn't find anything," said Momma.

"Well, we found us a spring out in the swamp," said Grandpa. He built a box out of wood, then took it back to the swampy area and put it down in the hole so it wouldn't cave in. That was our water spring. We could

31

use it to wash clothes and cook, but it didn't taste too good. It was more of a swamp water spring than a true well, so we'd need something else to drink.

Grandpa and I went out looking for drinking water, carrying three gallon jugs. About half a mile away through the woods, there was a little farmhouse. It was facing a gravel road and had a mailbox out front. The house was well-kept. We walked up to it and peered in the windows.

"Do you see anybody, Grampaw?" I asked.

"Naw," he said, then yelled, "Anybody home?"

There was no answer. We saw a well house in the side yard, so we went over to it and lowered the bucket until we heard a splash, then pulled it up, filled with water. We filled our jugs and started walking back toward our shack.

Taking a different route back, we found that it was a shorter distance than the way we'd come. After crossing a small wooded area, we came out into a field where I saw something I'd never seen before.

There in the field was a man plowing his cotton field with two oxen. They were the largest animals I'd ever seen. Even though I'd seen cows before, these were much bigger. The oxen had yokes around their necks and moved very slowly in unison. It amazed me that they made exactly the same movements at the same time. I had seen mules and horses plow before, but never oxen. I thought, "A child could watch this all day long!"

But the oxen were not all that fascinated me. The farmer driving them had skin as black as night. Even when I was in the orphans' home, I'd never seen a Negro before. It confused me, and I thought, "Why is his skin so black and mine is white?" I could not understand it. The man was probably in his mid-sixties, and had almost all gray hair. He was well-built, with nice clothes and shoes, and he spoke very slowly. He seemed to be a very nice, hard-working man.

As I stood and watched, the Negro man said very few words to the oxen. They seemed to know exactly what to do at all times. My grandpa yelled out to him, "We stopped at your well to get some water. We done moved into the old house back in them woods, and the spring water ain't worth drinkin'. We'd like to stop by once a day and fill up our jugs, if that's okay with you."

The old farmer looked at us for a long time. We must've been a sight, me still covered with chicken crap, and my old grandpa, whose reputation always preceded him. He finally said, "That's okay for now, but y'all need yo' own well, or to get yo' spring cleaned out." Even I could tell he didn't want us using his well. Everybody in the county knew my grandpa, who was known to steal anything he could get his hands on. The farmer said to him, "If y'all need some help cleanin' out yo' spring, I'll be glad to help."

"Naw, we can take care of cleanin' out that spring ourselves," said

Grandpa. "But we grateful for the offer, anyway."

I found out later in life that the farmer was the grandson of a slave. He had inherited this farm from his father, who'd inherited it from the former slave that was *his* father. When his master had died, he'd left the property to his slave, who then became free. It was rare to find a colored man in the 1930's who owned his own farm, especially in Mississippi.

We hadn't seen a woman around, so I guessed that this man's wife had died, and he lived all alone. I never met this old Negro gentleman again, but his face stayed with me all my life. In years to come, whenever I'd see the kids' movie *Br'er Rabbit*, or any others featuring an old black man with gray hair making children laugh, I'd think of this man.

Leaving the farmer behind, we crossed the cotton field toward our half-finished house. We passed through another small thicket of trees, then on to another small farm field. In this field was a small pea pen, where the old Negro man kept his black-eyed peas. It was completely full of them. My grandpa looked inside and said, "What in the world is this nigga gon' do with all them black-eyed peas? Ain't nobody can eat that many black-eyed peas."

We finally arrived back at our shack. We had only walked about a mile through the fields, creeks, woods and bushes, but it had worn me out. Little did I know we had hardly any food and no money.

That night, we ate possum and mush. The possum was left over from the day before. It reminded me of the Jell-O I'd eaten at the orphan's home. Jell-O would shake if you just touched it. This day-old possum was the same. The grease in the pan would shake when you touched the pan. I did not like possum, especially cold possum. I ate a few bites because I was so hungry. The mush actually felt good in my little tummy because it was warm, after being cooked in boiling water. Dub never complained, but I could tell that neither he nor my mother were happy about eating that cold possum.

We were hungry most of the time we lived at this place. Many times I went to bed without eating, as did my mother and brother Dub. Even though we'd brought some chickens with us, we had no food for them and they began to leave, disappearing through the woods. Hawks and fox probably ate most of them because they were gone within a few days. That also took away our source of eggs to eat.

Grandpa would disappear for days, then show up all of a sudden. One day, he brought home some black-eyed peas. We put a sheet down on the floor and he dumped a bushel of unshelled black-eyed peas on it. We shelled the peas, and that brought our menu up to possum, mush and black-eyed peas. There was no place to fish, so we didn't even have any fish.

We did have a little excitement around this place. My mother had an

33

old Victrola, a record player. It stood about three feet high. That Victrola was her pride and joy. She took especially good care of it. One problem with it: the needles would wear out in no time, and we had no money to buy more. The records for it were huge, and you had to use a crank on the side of the machine to wind it up. That was my job, to keep the machine wound up. She would listen to the records whenever she could get a new needle. One I especially liked was *A Tisket, A Tasket* by a lady named Ella Fitzgerald. I used to go around singing it all the time.

One day, some women came over. They were about my mother's age, and I think they were her relatives. They brought some records to play. "Ooh, Lawdy, we best send Dub outside to play," one of them said.

"Yes, Dub, you better go outside to play," echoed my mother.

"I don't think Joe's old enough to understand them dirty records, but Dub sho' would."

Dub went on outside, but I got to stay behind with the ladies. After all, it was my job to wind up the Victrola.

Most of the records were popular music of the time: Jimmy Rogers, who was known as the "Blue Yodeler", Roy Acuff, things like that. They weren't "dirty"; they were more or less country records. The one they said was dirty was named "Sweet Violette." It went like this:

"She is covered all over from head to toes
With sweet violets
Covered all over from head to her
Sweet violet"[1]

When it would get to this part, they would turn the volume up loud. They stayed all afternoon, laughing and listening to the records. When they left, nobody else came to visit us for a little while.

One day, Grandpa took Dub and me out to get some milk. Not from a store, but from a farmer's cow who was grazing in the field. We went out to that pasture with a bucket to milk her. "Watch out for them cow pies, Joe Abb," said Dub, just as I was about to step in a big one.

"Dub, you hold the cow still, and I'll milk her," said Grandpa.

Dub went around to the cow's head and tried to hold onto her bridle, but she wasn't having that. She tossed her head and walked away from us.

"Hold 'er still!" said Grandpa.

"I'm tryin', Grampaw, but she won't stay!"

"Wants to be fed, first," observed Grandpa.

"But ain't she eatin' the grass?" I said.

"Yeah, boy, but she wants grain," said Grandpa.

We tried several times to get some milk from the cow, but never could get her to stand still long enough. Eventually, we had to return to the shack with an empty pail.

A couple of weeks later, a teenage boy showed up. He was my mother's half-brother, Ben, and I just fell in love with him. Ben was sixteen years old, and wore a bright red shirt. Older people at the time thought men who wore bright red shirts were a little squirrelly. I thought it was cool, though, and so did most of the teenagers.

When Ben showed up, he had his girlfriend in tow with him. My mother didn't like that.

"You get that slut out of my house," she told Ben.

"But, Sister, where's she supposed to stay?"

"I don't care. She ain't comin' in my house."

The girl ended up staying in the woods near the house, under an old tarpaulin. I'd look out from time to time and see her moving around between the trees.

Ben had been down in the Mississippi delta, in the rich farmland. He said he was "pickin' cotton and makin' *good* money."

"What's good money?" asked my mother.

"Why, they payin' a penny a pound, and I can pick two hundred pounds a day." Two dollars a day was big money during the Depression.

Once Ben showed up, we started eating hot biscuits with sawmill gravy and, boy, was it good! Uncle Ben would show me his money. He had a huge money clip to hold it all in one big wad. My eyes would bug out just to look at that big ol' wad of money.

"Uncle Ben, I wanna be just like you," I told him. Get me a bright red shirt and a money clip. He also had a big pocket watch on a long chain. "Tell me the time, Uncle Ben," I used to say, just to see him pull that big watch out of his pocket. I thought he had everything, but he was really just like the rest of the poor, white trash at that time. A few dollars in his pocket, and a red shirt on his back.

Uncle Ben was one of the funniest people I've ever met. He would do this crazy kind of buck dance where he would point here and there around the room. I always looked wherever he pointed, so he was always making me laugh because nothing was there. Ben was also kind-hearted, and would give you that red shirt right off his back. But his time with us was short-lived. He stayed less than a week before disappearing. I never saw him again.

Chapter 9
Gone Again

After Ben left, things kept getting worse and worse for us. We moved again to another farmhouse of about the same type. A man by the name of Mr. Turnipseed said we could live on his farm if we would pick cotton for him. He would pay us to pick the cotton and give us an old shack to live in.

This was about the time for the third cotton picking. You pick cotton three times. The first one is good, then on the second picking there's still some left. By the time it's picked the third time, there's nothing much left but scraps, or what we called the "strippings." Scraps were all we had, anyway, and that's all that was left for us to pick.

We had sold most of our things to get some money while we were living at the McClure house. The weather was starting to get cold when we moved to the Turnipseed shack. All those Mississippi farmhouses must've been built by the same guy at the same time, because every one of them was the same, inside and out. There were always big cracks in the floor. At this house, Dub had an Indian-head penny he was really proud of. In those days, a penny would buy you a stick of candy. He was showing it to me one day, when it fell on the floor and rolled into one of those cracks.

"Dang it all! there goes my penny!" he said.

"Can't we crawl under the house and find it?" I asked him.

"I'm sho' gon' try," he said as he scrambled outside to go under the house and look for his lost treasure.

When he finally came out, I asked him "Did you find it, Dub?"

"Naw." Dub cried for days over that lost penny. He would continue to look for it every day we lived in that house, but he'd never find it.

We were still hungry living here, and my grandfather decided to set a trap to catch some food. He got a steel trap that only had one side working, and nailed it to a fence post with about a two-foot chain. The trap was baited with chicken entrails. When we went back the next day, he'd caught a hawk in the trap. The hawk was still alive, with both his feet caught in the trap. They'd gotten stuck when he'd swooped down to grab those chicken entrails with both talons, like hawks do. He was just hanging there from the trap, where it was nailed to the fence.

As we approached, he saw us and started screeching and flapping his wings. He was a very large bird, solid white underneath his wings and on the belly. On top he was brown and reddish, with a few black spots. The hawk was so strong that he'd almost get airborne, even with the weight of that trap pulling him down. He'd get a couple of feet up in the air, then the chain would run out and snatch him back down. After falling back into the fence post and barbed wire, he'd try again, get airborne, then fall back down. The screech he was making was almost like a hoot owl, but a little different. It was a real screaming voice. He started bleeding all over from falling into that barbed wire.

Curiously, the chicken entrails that had been used to bait the trap were lying there on the ground. I supposed when he got caught in that trap, he'd lost his appetite. Grandpa threw a toe sack over the hawk's head, then cut its head off. We took the big bird home and boiled it, then fried it up in the fireplace. I've never had tougher meat than that hawk.

I don't remember any of us ever picking any cotton for Mr. Turnipseed. That's probably why we didn't live there for long. The nights were beginning to get cold. Temperature was the only way I could tell about what month it was. I did not have any shoes, so when the weather got cold, my feet would turn blue. They would hurt, too, and I cried for hours.

This old two-room house was in the middle of a ten-acre cotton field. From the front of the house, all you could see was cotton. The land was not rich here, so even the best of the cotton crop was not good. By this time, it was down to the strippings and there wasn't much left to pick. The fields were largely brown with little spots of white here and there.

Cotton also surrounded the back of the house, but way back, past the cotton, you could see some woods. I longed for the beautiful view we'd had at the Choctaw Creek. This place looked like everything was lost. A gravel road looped in front of the house about 600-700 feet, overlooking the cotton field. Then it turned right and passed close by another sharecropping house about 400 feet away from ours.

There was a path leading from the side of our house, through the cotton field, to this other house. At the other house was where we got our water. This sharecropper had a large well, and did not mind our getting water there. After all, everything belonged to Mr. Turnipseed; the houses, the wells and the fields. I saw him once. He was a tall, thin, bespectacled man about forty years old.

My mother made good friends with the people at the sharecropping house by the well. They were about her age. She and Dub would always go together to get the water, and would stay to talk for long periods of time.

One day, around noon, we were all sitting on the small front porch looking out over the cotton patch. Lolly and Joe Woodard were inside, taking their afternoon nap. Coming down the road, making a terrible racket, was an old, small truck. The truck had no top. There was an empty wooden bed on the back, just a windshield sticking up and a seat across the front with two men in it. It misfired, backfired and made pitiful sounds. There must not've been a muffler on it, so you could hear it for miles. It passed our house, went down the road a short distance, then turned around and came back.

"Lawda mercy, lookathat!" said Grandpa.

"What is it, Grampaw?" I asked.

He laughed. "I don't rightly know. Probably a 1920 Model-T. I don't think it's gon' make it past the well house!"

Just as the truck came hitting and missing down the gravel road, my mother and Dub got all the buckets and told my grandfather, "We goin' down to get some water from the well." They started down the path to the well house.

"Y'all best stay and watch this show," he laughed as they disappeared down the road.

We heard the truck's motor almost stop as it was passing the well house. Then it started getting louder and louder before fading away in the distance. Grandpa said, "By God, that piece o' shit made it!"

We sat on the porch a while longer. "I wonder who in the hell them crazy people was," he said. He and I were waiting on my mother and Dub to get back with the water so she could cook some food for supper. We were very hungry.

All of a sudden, Grandpa grabbed his shotgun, fired up in the air and ran for the well house. I'd never heard so much screaming and hollering in my life. All I could hear was, "You goddamn sumbitch! I'll shoot yer goddamn ass!"

I ran toward the well house behind Grandpa. He was still shooting and cursing. When we finally got there, the people who lived there would not come outside. Grandpa said, "Come outside and tell me where Canny is!"

Grandpa had figured out that the guy driving that old, beat-up truck was the same one who used to come and visit my mother in the red truck, when we were back at Choctaw. They had run off together, after prearranging for her to meet him when that truck went down the road past our house and turned around. Brother Dub had put all the pieces together, and had figured out this was happening, so he kept close to his mother, just like at the orphanage. He'd jumped into the back of that truck with our mother.

Well, it was getting late in the evening. Here we were, Grandpa, myself, Lolly and baby Joe Woodard, alone in the house. My mother was gone from my life again. We were all at a loss for words, and went to bed early, without any supper. Lolly usually slept with my mother, and I with Grandpa, but she slept with me this night, and Grandpa slept with baby Joe. All I could hear all night was Grandpa cussing and the baby crying. What were we to do now?

Chapter 10
The Journey

The next morning, we must have eaten something for breakfast, but I don't remember what it was. Grandpa was busy, and Lolly and I played outside. The weather had been cool, but we were enjoying a little Indian summer right now, and it wasn't so bad.

Late in the afternoon, Grandpa said, "Come on. We gon' over to the Mileses' house. Y'all gon' stay there 'til I find yo' momma."

I'd never heard of the Mileses before, but they were cousins of my mother. That was who Lolly would go to stay with from time to time. Grandpa took a toe sack and cut little holes in each of the bottom corners and a big hole in the top. Then he put baby Joe Woodard in the toe sack with his little legs dangling out the holes and slung the sack over his shoulder, across his back. Baby Joe didn't seem to mind, and Grandpa said this was easier than carrying the baby in his arms. We children didn't have any coats or shoes, so Lolly was just wearing a little cotton dress, and I had on some bib overalls with no shirt.

We set off across the cotton fields, Lolly and I dragging along well behind our grandfather. Finally, we reached the woods. Grandpa turned to us and said, "Now, y'all young'uns stay on the trail in these here woods, and y'all won't get lost."

"Okay, Grampaw," I said. Our feet were pretty tough from never wearing shoes, but this walk was still rough on us. We lagged farther and farther behind Grandpa.

By this time, we were pretty deep in the woods, and Grandpa was out of sight. We stayed on the trail, so we wouldn't get lost. Before long, Lolly was also lagging behind me, but we pressed on. After about an hour of walking, we came up on an old house that was in the same sad shape as the one we'd just left. There was no road that I could see, just an old shack house sitting out in a large, cleared piece of ground. I was so tired, I sat down on a bucket in the yard to wait for Lolly. I could see her coming behind me, a couple hundred feet down the trail.

While I was waiting, a little boy about my age came out of the shack. We just stood and looked at each other. He smiled, and I smiled back. His skin was dark, like the old farmer I'd seen in the field, but the strangest thing to me was that he had no clothes on. I would later find out that it was customary in that part of the country at that time for little Negro boys not to wear any clothes until they were about nine years old, but I'd never heard of such a thing before.

Another odd thing was that his private was sticking straight out. He said to me, "You, you wanna play?"

I said, "Naw, I'm waitin' for my little sister."

Just about that time, Lolly showed up and said, "I got to rest, Joe Abb. I can't walk no more."

She was only 4½ years old, so we just sat down to let her rest. She kept looking at the little Negro boy with his private sticking straight out and finally said, "What's he want?"

"I don't know," I said.

About that time, a Negro lady came out of the house and said, "Where yer chi'ren mommuh?" The lady was large and fat, with a red bandana on her head. She wore a clean-looking dress with no shoes, and looked to be about the same age as my momma.

"I don't know," I said. "We lookin' for her. We goin' to the Mileses' house."

She seemed to know where this was, and said, "Y'all chi'ren hungry?"

I said, "Yeah!" She went inside the house and brought out two biscuits with a large piece of fatback in between the biscuits. I guess she could tell we hadn't had anything to eat all day.

We quickly ate the biscuits and fatback, then split a large glass of buttermilk she brought. After that, I felt like I could walk another five miles.

The nice colored lady asked, "What y'all chi'ren doin' down heah? Y'all ought to be home."

I explained again, "We goin' to the Mileses' house, to stay with them 'til my grampaw can find our momma."

"Well, it's down the trail an' 'cross that gravel road, 'bout a mile. It's gon' be dark soon, so y'all bes' git on down there."

Sis and I started walking again, hoping we could find the Miles house. The sweet lady stood there and watched us until we went out of sight down the trail. I learned later that the colored family who lived there were sawmill workers.

After walking for what seemed like forever, we finally caught up to our grandfather and baby Joe Woodard. They were sitting on a log along the path, waiting for Sis and me. "'Bout time y'all showed up," said Grandpa, quietly. Baby Joe was fast asleep in the toe sack, feet and head hanging out, not making a sound.

We walked a short distance with him, and came out of the woods into a large field on the side of a hill. Looking down the hill was a gravel road and a white "shotgun" house. A shotgun house was called that because it was built with two rooms on either side of a central hallway that ran down the middle of the house, from the front door to the back. You could shoot a shotgun through the front doorway of the house, and the buckshot wouldn't hit a thing before it passed out the back door.

It was starting to get dark, and we walked toward the house. There was a picket fence across the front of the yard. When we arrived at the house, there was a woman, a man and a little boy my age. The man and woman were about my momma's age; that was Mr. and Mrs. Miles. The little boy's name was Billy, and he was their son.

Sis and I were so tired, our little legs were nearly worn out. It seemed like we'd walked a thousand miles. Mrs. Miles washed our feet and put us both to bed. I slept with Billy. Even though we'd walked all that distance without shoes, my last thought before drifting off was still, "Where is my momma? I'm always lookin' for my momma."

Chapter 11
Trouble Again

We awoke the next morning to the smell of coffee. I'd smelled coffee before, but never in the morning. Mrs. Miles had breakfast ready. It was the most food I'd seen in months, ever since leaving the home. We had eggs, side meat, gravy, biscuits – what more could you want? All the milk you could drink, and the best thing was a playmate for me.

After breakfast, Grandpa left to look for our momma. Although I would remember him my whole life, I would never see him again. After he left, we stayed with the Miles family. Their son, Billy, was a follower, and I was a natural leader. After Grandpa left, we went out on the back porch to play. There was a large, galvanized washtub sitting there, upside-down.

"Why's that tub upside-down?" I asked him.

"They's two possums under there," he said. "Daddy caught 'em."

"Well, what's he gon' do with 'em?" I asked.

"I reckon sell 'em," he said.

This triggered my memory, and I suddenly knew what we had to do. "Well, then, we need to help him get 'em ready for the market."

"How we gon' do that?" he said.

"We need to cut off their tails." I'd seen my grandfather do this with the bulldog pups he'd sold at the market in Ackerman, so I thought this was automatically what needed to be done to prepare animals for sale. "Go get yo' daddy's axe. We gon' cut the tails off these possums."

Billy went off and came back with an axe.

"Now, you grab the tails while I move this washtub, and hold onto 'em, and I'll keep the tub so they can't get out. Once you get them tails out and the tub on top, we can cut their tails off."

"Okay," said Billy. I could tell he was sold on this new adventure.

While my plan sounded really good to us, these two possums didn't want two six-year-old boys cutting their tails off. We finally got one of their tails out from under the washtub. I was just getting the axe ready when Billy said, "Oh-oh!"

Billy couldn't hold the tub and the tail at the same time, and the two possums came out from under there and hauled ass back into the woods.

43

We never saw them again.

"Well, that's just great, Billy. Now, we really gon' get it!" The first morning I was there, and I was already in trouble.

Mrs. Miles hit the ceiling when she found out we'd let those possums loose. "Just you wait 'til Mister Miles gets home tonight, Joe Abb Overby!" she said.

She scared the living daylights out of me, and I knew I was going to be out of another place to live. When Mr. Miles came in that evening, she told him everything. "You get that damn Overby boy outta my house now!" she said. "He's only been here for ten hours, and he done already made a bad, criminal child outta my son! If he grows up 'round here with our son, they gon' both wind up in the state reformatory school! You start lookin' for a place. He is not stayin' here! He done already been kicked outta the Methodist Orphans' Home 'cause he was so damn mean. He is not goin' to send *my* son to prison. Now get him to heck outta my house!"

I started to cry. I looked at Mrs. Miles and said, "All we was gon' do was cut their tails off. After all, it was Billy's idea." Billy didn't say a word to defend himself, but nobody believed me over their own son.

"Now, Joe, don't you worry none about it. They's just a coupla ol' possums. We can catch some more. Just don't try that again. Now, y'all boys get washed up for supper, you hear?"

"Yessuh."

Despite my bad start, I stayed with the Miles family for about a month. I didn't really like it there, but Mrs. Miles was good to me. She fed me and gave me a warm bed to sleep in. The whole month, I kept Billy in trouble. He would've followed me straight into the fire, if I'd asked him to. I spent all my time with Billy, and barely noticed Lolly or baby Joe Woodard there.

Mrs. Miles would get mad at us and say, "Billy Miles, if y'all don't behave, Santa Claus gon' bring y'all a bag of switches!" All I knew about Santa Claus was what little I'd heard in the orphans' home. They didn't want us to think too much about getting presents for Christmas, because all we had was what people donated to us. So her threat meant little to me, but it seemed to work on Billy, even if only for a short time.

One morning, I heard a noise I'd heard once before. Billy and I ran out on the front porch, and there was that crazy old truck without a cab, and with a wooden bed on it, driving right up to the house! You could hear it long before you could see it. Loud noise, lots of smoke, up the gravel road it came. They stopped it, with a loud backfire, just short of hitting the picket fence.

A loud voice shouted out, "Get them damn young'uns in this truck!

We got a long ways to go."

Mrs. Miles was only too happy to put me, baby Joe and Lolly in the truck, and down the old gravel road we went. None of us kids knew where we were going, but to me, riding in that beat-up, old truck was the right thing to do. I loved it.

There were three people in the front part of the truck, and their last name was Franklin. The oldest was a man in about his 30's, with two young teenage boys that I thought must be his sons. I kept looking at the older man; I'd seen him somewhere before, but I could not remember where.

We rode in that truck for about two and a half hours, which was a long time on a bumpy, gravel road. The only time I'd ever even seen a paved road was that brief time I was in Jackson, when I'd run away from the orphanage. I don't think there was another one in the whole state of Mississippi!

Finally, it dawned on me where I'd seen the truck's driver before. He was that man who used to come to our house in the red dump truck! I thought, "He's that guy who let me drive his truck when we lived at Choctaw."

We finally got to a house with a dirt yard, pulled into the yard and the engine backfired several times. I thought for sure it would catch fire before it stopped. We got out and walked toward the house. I looked up and coming out the front door was my momma! She looked just the same, with the same old flour-sack skirt and blouse she'd always worn. Momma used to sew her own clothes, and had even held a job sewing for the welfare at the time I'd been in the orphanage. Dub told me about it because he used to go with her and sit by her feet while she worked.

I ran up to my momma and hugged her really tight, but she just looked at me and walked away. Dub was standing behind her. I hadn't seen him in a while, either, since he'd been with our momma. Finally, I put my arms around my brother. I really loved Dub; he would always protect me. Like our mother, though, and he didn't say anything to me. He hadn't always been that way. He'd gotten like that after the shooting that had put our father in prison.

Whether he showed it or not, I knew that Dub loved me. What mattered now was that we were all together again – all except John, that is. He was still in the orphanage in Jackson. I thought about him from time to time, but didn't know if I'd ever see him again. My memories of him were starting to fade.

Chapter 12
The Wild Life

Here we were, almost all together again, at my mother's lover's house near McCool, Mississippi. His name was Willy Franklin, but everybody called him Ben. He had a small farm, with some chickens and a large sorghum patch. That's what's used to make blackstrap molasses. His three boys helped him work the farm. It was fall now, time to harvest the sorghum.

A few days after arriving at the Franklin house, I went on a wagon with a team of mules with his boy, Wilbur, down a dirt road into a field and started loading sorghum cane. Wilbur showed me how to load it. He was about twelve or thirteen years old, and had been doing this for years. We got the sorghum as high as we could on the wagon, then tied ropes around the cane to the wagon so it wouldn't fall off. Then we climbed up on top of the cane, about fifteen feet high, and drove off.

"Where we goin', Wilbur?" I asked.

"To the cook-off," he said.

"What's that?"

"That's where they make the molasses."

"How they make it?"

"You'll see. But you gotta remember a couple of things, Joe Abb."

"What's that?"

"Don't get too close to the grinder, and don't drink any of that juice there."

"Juice?"

"Yeah; you'll see. Just remember not to drink any of it."

"Okay."

When we pulled up the wagon at the cook-off, I was really excited. It was just like a big party. Lots of older men were standing around under this big, tin-roofed open shed with no sides on it. One was sitting on a stool, just stroking the juice from the cane in a long pan that must've been about twenty feet long and four feet wide. The pan had compartments in it. There was a fire underneath it, and sweet-smelling vapors were rising from the pan. The man was an expert at making sorghum molasses, and the cook-off belonged to him. Since he owned it, he got a percentage of the amount of sorghum molasses he made.

The other thing that caught my eye was a small donkey, a jackass. He was hitched to a long pole leading from the grinder, over in another part of the shed. The grinder itself looked like an old washing machine wringer, but a lot bigger and made out of steel. Men were feeding the sticks of cane into the grinder, and the juice would run through a barrel at the bottom of the grinder. Someone would carry this juice by hand over to the pans that were cooking the juice. The donkey would walk slowly around and around, hitched to this pole to keep the grinder going.

Our wagon pulled up to the grinder. Wilbur and I fed the cane sticks into the grinder. "Careful, Joe Abb, don't get too close to it. Could lose a hand, or a finger, like ol' Bob over there."

I looked over, and there was a man missing a finger. "He did that in the grinder?" I asked.

"Yep. So don't get too close to it. Fact, you just go over there and wait while I do this." I guess Wilbur didn't want to be responsible for what might happen to me, since I was not even six years old yet.

I wandered over to where the juice was coming out of the grinder into a big wooden barrel. I kept looking at that sweet cane juice in the barrel. It was a light greenish color, and smelled sweet, fresh and natural. Flies were buzzing all around it, so I knew it had to be sweet. I finally couldn't resist it any longer. Grabbing a metal cup I found in a corner, I dipped myself out a taste. It was so sweet and so good, I kept doing it again and again. Not only was it sweet, it had a fresh, green taste to it that kept me coming back for more. One of the men saw me and said, "Boy, don't be drinkin' that juice! Make ya sick!" I was more careful after that, but kept sneaking cups of the juice whenever I could get away with it.

Late in the afternoon, we finished up at the cook-off, and Wilbur and I headed back toward the Franklin house. We had a good supper, then washed our feet and went to bed. There never seemed to be any shortage of food here; that molasses business must have paid pretty well. I slept in the same bed as Wilbur that night. He'd taught me so much this day, I thought he knew everything. After all, he drove a team of mules and wagon all day long. We both fell asleep fast after working hard all day.

About an hour after falling asleep, I woke up with really bad stomach cramps. I had to get to the bathroom, and now! This house didn't have any indoor plumbing, either, so I had to make it to the outside john. Before I could even get out of the bed, I lost control of my bowels and crapped all over the bed, and all over Wilbur.

"Dammit, Joe Abb, what the…" he said. "Aw, I ain't gon' sleep with you no more! I *told* you not to drink that juice, and you did it, anyway, didn't you? You gon' hafta wash them quilts, y'know!"

47

Wilbur went in and slept on the floor in another room, and I spent most of that night in the outside john. That sorghum cane juice really flushed me out.

The next morning, when we got up for breakfast, Ben told me, "Joe Abb, don't you drink no more of that cane juice today. And remember to use the bathroom before you go to bed." I felt like the most disturbed child they'd ever met. It seemed that every place I lived, I did something to start a very bad relationship right up front.

We continued working the sorghum fields and the cook-off with the team of mules and wagon. When we got home that night, somebody had washed the quilts on our bed.

I never did like the Franklin place too much. There was always plenty to eat there, but not necessarily for us. Wilbur got to where he picked on me all the time, so our friendship didn't last very long. Lolly, Dub and I hung together, and always got the leftovers, which wasn't much. They'd let us know in a lot of ways that we were intruding on their house. When we'd try to get in near the fireplace, they'd push us back and say, "This ain't your place, it's mine." When Momma would make a cake, Wilbur would get to lick the icing pan, never us. They would make me get the firewood, saying, "You livin' here in my house."

Days were still warm, but nights were really cold here. I could always tell the weather by my feet getting cold. No shoes, still. It must have been October, because I remember getting a pair of cowboy gloves from my mother. They had long tassels made of leather strings hanging down the back side of them. I remember Dub telling me that they were for my birthday, and I knew my birthday was in October. I'd wear my fancy gloves, and we'd use sticks for guns to play cowboys and Indians, just like those in the movies I'd seen back at the orphans' home.

Some days at this time would be sunny and warm, then late in the evening the temperature would drop fast and my feet would turn blue from the cold. My feet ached so badly from the cold I would go inside the old farmhouse and push and shove the Franklin boys aside to get close to the fireplace. Once my feet would start warming up, they'd hurt twice as bad. Dub got me a bucket of cold water and made me put my feet in it to get them about normal. Then the hurt would go away, and the fireplace would warm me up.

It was each man for himself at the Franklin house, and the devil for the crowd. My mother took care of Mr. Franklin and let her own kids do without. Maybe she was afraid of being kicked out. I really did not understand this situation.

During the warm part of the day, I would play outside. There seemed to always be lots of men coming around, driving old cars and trucks. They would not stay too long. They were there to buy sorghum molasses, and my job was to fill up the cans with the molasses and put the lid on them. We had three or four 50-gallon wooden barrels sitting on wooden sawhorses out behind the house. When somebody wanted molasses, I'd go out to the barrels and shoo away about a hundred flies that would have lit on the knob. Then I'd turn that wooden spout, and the molasses would run out into the buckets. If you didn't have your own bucket, it cost you five cents more a gallon. Most people had their own bucket or jug of some sort. My mother would handle the money part of things while I was getting the molasses.

If it was a warm and sunny day, the flies around those molasses barrels would increase to about three hundred. Nobody seemed to mind. While all this was going on, my mother would sit on the far end of the front porch, on the other side of the house from where I got the molasses. There was an old, beat-up rocker there on the porch, and that's where she usually sat, fanning flies. Even though the nights were cold, it was always hot there in the daytime. Momma was constantly watching everything, but not saying a word.

I was busy as a bee taking care of the molasses. I liked to be in charge, and would work my ass off. My mother would always go out to the car to get the money. Sometimes, Mr. Franklin would be seen a distance away, either at the barn or chopping firewood at the woodpile on the other side of the house. There was always a lot of traffic, the whole time we were there. People sure did use a lot of molasses around there!

One Sunday, a lot of Momma's relatives were coming over. "Y'all boys go out and catch me a couple of them chickens to cook for dinner – get the roosters, 'cause the hens lay eggs. We got plenty of roosters."

Wilbur and I chased a couple of roosters all over the yard for what seemed like forever, and finally hemmed one up under the house. "You try to feed 'im, then we'll grab 'im," said Wilbur.

I threw some corn on the ground to get the rooster out where we could get him. When he came out to eat it, we pounced on him. Between the two of us, we caught him, but he scratched and clawed both of us pretty good before we got him. Momma grabbed him from us and wrung his neck to kill him, then set about plucking his feathers out to get him ready for the frying pan.

She'd already made a coconut cake the day before. She actually went to the general store in McCool and bought a coconut. When she cracked it open, we got to drink the juice from it – and it didn't give me the runs, like that sorghum cane juice had done. Momma grated the coconut and made the prettiest white coconut cake you've ever seen. I could hardly wait to taste it. She even let me lick the pan and eat some of the icing.

The relatives all came by, and we had a big feast. I had to tell everybody that I had caught one of the chickens. Afterward, we all had a piece of that good coconut cake, then everybody just sat around on the front porch, talking and digesting our dinner. Several of the men were playing horseshoes in the front yard.

A couple of boys, about 18 and 19 years old, stopped by the house to buy some molasses. They were supposed to be friends of the Franklins. They also each wanted a haircut. Mr. Franklin's oldest boy, Orville, was about the same age as these boys, and he would cut people's hair for fifteen cents. Lots of men and boys came by there to get their hair cut.

While all this was going on, somebody else drove up in an old, beat-up truck, walked over to Mr. Franklin and started talking to him. Then, he left. I thought this was kind of odd.

When the man had left, Mr. Franklin said, "Boys, bring out the barber stool. Let's get these two boys a haircut so they can get on home."

He sent one of his boys on an errand in the barn. Mr. Franklin said to the two boys, "Y'all got the money for the haircut and the other?"

The boys said, "Hell, yes! We come here to buy, we ain't come here to talk no bull!"

The Franklin boys came back with two pint bottles, but they weren't filled with molasses. About that time, both boys had finished their haircuts and were standing up. Mr. Franklin said, "Y'all boys done been so good, got haircuts, and all. We got some special hair tonic we bought from Sears and Roebuck. Just got it in from Memphis, Tennessee by order three weeks ago. Just got here. Sit down in this chair and we'll give y'all some free hair tonic. It smells good an' jus' makes the girls chase hell outta ya."

The boys paid him, and were going to get their free hair tonic. That was a big deal, to give them some free tonic on their heads. They were happy as pigs in cracked corn about the tonic. They both sat down, and the two Franklin boys stood behind them to put on the tonic. They switched bottles and poured about a quart of sorghum molasses on their heads. Then Mr. Franklin and his boys said, "Get yer goddamn ass outta here, and don't come back! We know who to hell sent y'all here!"

The two boys ran down the road, pausing only long enough to pick up their pint bottles and take them with them. There they were, running down the road with sorghum molasses running down their faces and backs, a swarm of flies following each one.

Mr. Franklin and his boys were laughing like crazy, and he said, "I'd like to be there when them bastards take their first drink of that!"

I didn't know what had just happened, so I asked Dub that evening. As usual, he explained everything to me. "Joe Abb, the Franklins sell moonshine whiskey here. Them boys was sent out here by the sheriff to get evidence about it."

"They was?"

"Uh-huh. Remember that other man who come by to talk to Mister Franklin an' then left?"

"Yeah."

"Well, he come by here to warn him about them boys. So Mister Franklin told his boys to only put enough 'shine in them bottles so's they could smell it, then to piss in the bottle to fill it up and put the cap on."

"So that's why he had them boys pour the molasses over their heads?"

"Yep, so they knowed he was onto 'em. But they grabbed them pint jars before they left, so's they'd have their 'evidence'."

"And it was mostly piss!"

"Yep. I tell you what, Joe Abb. They's lucky they didn't get hurt bad, 'cause squealin' on somebody sellin' shine'll git ya shot!"

"Does Momma know about all this?"

"You kiddin'? She's the one handles all the money!"

I'd just thought there'd been about to be a good fight fixin' to happen. Seemed like every time a bunch of boys got together, there would always be a fight. Many years later, Lolly's husband heard this story and said he knew the two boys involved; I think he was even related to them.

The day after our adventure with the two "revenuers", at about two o'clock in the afternoon, a nice-looking, shiny, two-tone car drove into the yard. It was green and white, and was different from all the others that would come by to buy "molasses." The car had one seat across the front that would seat about three people; there were a lot of these back in the 1930s. There was also a mother-in-law seat behind the cab. It faced backward and could be folded down when not in use. Two men were riding in the front seat of the car, and the mother-in-law seat was shut.

Both men got out of the car and walked toward the house. One was a bald-headed man with a ring of hair around the edges of his head, and he was wearing an old, corduroy hat with a bib on it. He stood about 5'10" and was slender. He was very neat and clean-shaven, with smooth hands. With a lot of self-confidence and good manners, he approached my mother. "Hello, Canny."

"I don't wanna talk to you," she said, continuing to look straight ahead.

Then, I heard him say something like, "I've come to get the boys."

She said, "Go on and take them kids, if you want, but don't talk to me."

The man walked over to me and said, "Son, do you remember me?"

Oddly enough, I didn't. In all the years he'd been away, it was always my mother I'd been looking for, never my father. Dub remembered him, and said, "Hey, Dad. Hey, Mistuh Perry." The other man was Jim Perry, my father's former business partner in the hotel and café.

I was excited just looking at the car. I'd never seen one so fancy. My dad picked me up and threw me up in the air, then said, "Dub and Joe Abb, I'm gon' take y'all with me."

That was fine with me, especially if that meant I got to ride in that car, but Dub wanted to stay with Momma. He ran over to her and said, "I'm stayin' with my mother." He had been with her all his life.

Dad was smooth, though, and he said to Dub, "Come stay a week or two. If you don't like it, I'll bring you right back to your mother."

Dub was staunchly against it. It took some talking to get him to go, but he finally decided to come along. For me, I was ready to ride. I'd had enough of being made to feel like an intruder in somebody else's house, and I was ready to try someplace new. Mr. Perry helped, too, by saying, "When we get to the gravel road, I'll even let you drive this damn car!"

Boy, that excited me. Let me drive a car? I was crazy about that! They put me, Dub and Sis Lolly in the mother-in-law seat and down the old dirt road we went. Dust was flying all over the place. I was happy as I could be to be riding in that back seat, but Dub was sad. He was thinking of leaving his mother, and just kept looking back as we pulled out of the yard. As we pulled away, our mother sat on the porch with her legs and bare feet hanging off the edge. She never waved or said anything. Never hugged us 'bye, just sat there looking straight ahead. Not a pretty sight, just sitting there, waiting for somebody to come by and buy some moonshine.

I had just turned six years old, and that was the last time I ever saw my mother.

Chapter 13
Natural Salesman

All three of us kids fell asleep in the mother-in-law seat on the way to Uncle Jim Perry's. It was dark when we got to his house. They woke me up and put me and Lolly to bed. We slept together that night. My dad had just gotten out of prison, and Uncle Jim Perry was his best friend.

The next morning, Dad and Uncle Jim got me up early and put me in a pickup truck with brother Dub. Uncle Jim drove us about sixty miles north to a town called Bruce, Mississippi. It was a sawmill town then, and still is today. Sixty miles in the 1930's on a gravel road was quite a haul. The road was Highway Number Nine, going north. Lolly stayed with the Perrys the rest of her life. My dad did not claim her as his, but you could line her up with all us boys, and we all looked just alike. We never had any doubt she was our sister.

Uncle Jim Perry and my dad had married first cousins. That's why we called him Uncle Jim and his wife Aunt Bessie. They raised my sister in Choctaw County, where we'd all started out.

After Uncle Jim dropped us off at Bruce, we saw very little of the Perrys. My dad was born and raised around Bruce. He knew almost everyone there. Since he'd just gotten out of prison, he had no money. His first wife and a pack of kids still lived around there. They had no use for him, since he had run off and left them to fend for themselves. I had half-brothers and half-sisters forty years older than me that I had never seen. Most of them did not want to be associated with us.

We had nothing. A gentleman named Wash Hughes let us live in one room of his rooming house. We had one bed, some nail cags to sit on and a pot-bellied stove to warm up the place and cook on. We were eating a lot of fried cornbread again.

The weather was really getting cold, especially now that we were a little farther north. I had shoes here, and some clothes to keep me warm. Where they'd come from, I don't know. We got welfare and food stamps, so we always had a little bit of food. Dub also told me that Dad had applied for his old-age pension. He was over 65 and had a broken hip that he'd injured when he fell off a small building doing some carpentry work. His old-age pension was $11 a month. Social Security had only been around for a couple of years, so he wasn't eligible to receive any money in that program.

Christmas came and went, and we didn't have money to buy any presents. There were Christmas trees all over town, but we didn't have one of those, either. The welfare people made sure we kids had stockings with an apple and an orange in them. I remember just after Christmas, smelling the strong scent of cedar as everybody put their old, dead Christmas trees out front for the garbage man.

We had to do something to get some more income, so my dad would put Dub and me out on the street corners around Bruce to sing for money. I was a pretty good singer, and so was Dub, but he was more shy. I loved to be in the spotlight. It helped a little, but this wasn't making us enough money to make ends meet, either.

Next, Dad made a peanut roaster from a ten-gallon steel drum. It had a handle on one end so he could turn it around. He'd take it down by the cotton gin in town, build a fire underneath it and turn it around and around until the peanuts were roasted.

There wasn't a lot of traffic near the cotton gin, though, so Dad went down to the grocery store and got a couple of cardboard boxes. He cut the bottom part out, and fitted it with a string that went around my neck. One for me, and one for Dub. He filled up each box with peanuts in little brown bags, and said, "Go git 'em boys! Sell, sell, sell! Sell those roasted peanuts!"

This was right down my alley. I hit the streets on a Saturday afternoon with all those sawmill workers with money in their pockets. I sold peanuts faster than my dad could parch them. I would not be gone over thirty minutes out on the streets before I was back for more peanuts. Dub only sold two packs of peanuts all day.

"Dub, why couldn't you sell more?" I asked him that afternoon.

"I don't know."

"Well, how'd you do it?"

"Well, I stood on the corner, where they could see me, and looked out across the street. Hardly nobody stopped."

"There's your problem! You got to *yell.*" It was true. Everyone could hear me all over town, yelling, "Get your *rooooasted* peanuts here!" I loved to walk up and down the streets and shout out, "Hot peanuts!" But Dub was shy, so he never could sell as many peanuts as I could.

There was a theater in downtown Bruce. I stood out in front of it and sold everyone going into the theater a bag of roasted peanuts. That did not go over too well with the owner of the theater. He was selling popcorn, and I was selling more peanuts than he was selling popcorn. He walked over to where I was standing and said, "You can't sell peanuts out here. This is my theater." He said it like thee-ay-ter, just like the matron at the home had done. "Get out of here, young'un!"

"Nawsuh. I'm sellin' peanuts, and that's what I'm supposed to be doin'," I told him.

"We gon' see about that!" he said and stormed off in a huff.

He returned in a few minutes with the town marshal. The marshal came up to me and said, "Boy, you can't sell no peanuts out in front of this man's business."

"Why not? It's a city street."

"'cause I'll put your li'l ass in the calaboose, that's why!" he said. That was what everybody called the jailhouse.

He continued, "You can sell anywhere 'cept in front of the theater. Now, get your butt down the street!"

The fact that he was wearing a pistol scared me a little. Back in those days, he didn't have on a uniform, just a sort of police hat, but he wore a pistol and a badge. I moved about a block back from the theater and still sold peanuts to people going to the movies. I'd ask them, "Y'all goin' to the picture show?"

If they said yes, I would say, "Peanuts taste better'n popcorn. Five cents a bag!"

Finally, the theater owner came down the block and made a deal with me. "If you don't sell peanuts within three blocks of this thee-ay-ter, I'll let you in to see the picture show free. How 'bout it?"

"Free? It's a deal!" From then on, every Saturday, I could see the 4:30 movies for free. My favorite was *Red Ryder and Little Beaver*, and it was usually something like that for the kids.

My dad, however, was not so enthusiastic about the deal I'd made. He told me, "I don't want you to go and see those movies no more. They're bad for young boys."

"Bad? But why?"

"Those women in the theater, they're showin' their knees an' they're kissin' men, right there on that screen in front of y'all little boys an' girls."

"But, Dad, I don't watch them movies. I like the ones with the cowboys an' Injuns!"

Of course, Dad was 65 years old, and could not change with the times. "Talkies" were just getting popular at that time, and it as unusual to have a theater in a small, jake-legging town like Bruce. There may have been one theater at the other end of the county, but that was it.

"I don't care, I don't want you seein' those movies. You hear me?"

"Yessuh." I may have agreed, but I didn't stop my Saturday afternoon ritual, just got sneakier about it.

One thing Dad always found the money for was a subscription to the

Grit newspaper. About once a month, a guy would walk down the road with a big satchel on his side, filled with newspapers. Whenever Dad got a new issue, he'd read it aloud to me and Dub. That was our connection to the world outside of our own.

"Set down here, boys," he said. "Let's find out what's goin' on in the world."

"What's that, Dad?" I asked.

"It's the *Grit* paper," he said, unfolding it. "It's important for you and Dub to know what's going on around the world."

"Why? How's it affect us if somebody does somethin' on the other side of the world?"

"Joe Abb, some stuff affects us," said Dub. "You remember that WPA project Grampaw was workin' on, back when we lived at Choctaw?"

"Yeah."

"That was somethin' that happened because of the Depression. President Roosevelt started it to give folks jobs, so they could feed their families."

"Well, there's lots of things happenin' now that will have a big effect on both of you," said Dad. "Just listen to this."

He proceeded to read us stories about President Roosevelt establishing an organization called the National Foundation for Infantile Paralysis. Then there was another about Austria recognizing the new government in Spain, and one about a guy named Hitler taking over in Germany. There was even a story about a new play opening on Broadway by a gentleman named Thornton Wilder. It was called *Our Town*. Even though Dad and Dub had to explain several of the news stories to me, I had to admit it was kind of interesting.

The first time I started to school was there in Bruce. I was a little late starting, what with moving from shack to shack in the old cotton fields with my mother. Even though I should've started the first grade in September, they agreed to let me start in January. It was hard, being behind the other kids, but I liked going to school and tried to keep up.

Dad came in one day and said, "Boys, we are movin'." Lord have mercy, again! We packed up what few things we had, and a man came by our rooming house with two mules pulling a wagon. We loaded up our things inside the open wagon and headed for our next home. It would end up being the place I would live for the longest time yet.

Chapter 14
Living Like Abe Lincoln

The man who helped us move was young, probably around 22 years old. His name was Mr. Cox. He had a boy my age, who he called "Dude."

Dude and I got along really well. We played and ran along beside the wagon, then would jump on it. It wasn't moving very fast. It took us three hours to move four miles outside of Bruce, where our new home would be. I told Dude a lot of stories that weren't true, but he believed them. He was another follower, like so many others I'd led astray through the years.

After a couple of hours on gravel roads, we came up to a large hill. It was one of the steepest in the area. The road wasn't kept very well on that hill, either. There were some washed-out gulleys from old wheel ruts that made it really hard for wagon and mules to get through. Once we got to the top, it was very steep on the other side, coming down. We finally got down the hill, then around a curve, and there was a log cabin. This was to be our new home.

The cabin had two rooms, and nobody had lived there for two or more years. At one time, there had been a sawmill about 500 feet behind the cabin. You could tell where it'd been because there was a huge pile of sawdust there. The pile was about 25 feet high. As the timber, mostly pine trees, was cut in that area, the sawmill would move deeper into the woods, probably a mile or so away.

The sawmill employed a large number of Negro workers, and a white man to be the boss. He and his wife would live in the log cabin and run the sawmill. Someone had arranged for my dad, Dub and me to live there free. Everywhere we lived, we lived free because we didn't have any money for rent.

Dude Cox came by a few more times to play with me when we first lived at the log cabin, but then he disappeared, and I never saw him again. I was told that his family were sawmill people, and they'd moved on.

We were really out in the woods by ourselves, here in the log cabin. You could not see any other houses around. There was a bigger log house a little farther down the road, owned by a family by the name of Mr. and Mrs. Raleigh. They had one daughter who lived with them at the time, and she was in her last year of high school.

The next house you came to belonged to Mr. and Mrs. Jim Easley. The Easleys were very good people. They had a daughter named Christine, who was about 16 or 17 years old, and she was in love. I would always see her and her boyfriend hugging and kissing and holding each other real tight. I was just a few months over six years old, and thought this was so strange. Of course, at my age and with all I'd been through, I didn't understand love. That was really the first time I recall seeing two people in love, walking and holding hands and everything.

When we first moved into the log cabin, we had very little food. The Raleighs and the Easleys gave us food. Mrs. Easley used to give us a gallon of cow's milk every night. I had to walk up that steep hill to get it. Sometimes I would get there early and have to wait until they milked the cows. James Selvin was Mr. Easley's youngest son. He and I would pour the milk into a separator. Then I would turn the crank really fast and the cream would come out one side, and the milk would come out the other.

Sometimes Mrs. Easley would let me churn. She had an old-fashioned churn. It had a wooden top with a hole in the middle. Something that looked like a broomstick stuck out through the hole. Inside the churn, two cross-pieces of wood screwed into the broomstick. I would churn up and down for what seemed like forever, and the cream would turn into butter. The churn was not old-fashioned at that time, it was what everybody used to make their butter.

We had plenty of corn meal, but if we hadn't gotten the milk from the Easleys, I don't know what we would've lived on. It was some distance down the road and up that large hill to their house. I really loved the Easleys. They had three grown children at home. The oldest was Wayne, then there was Christine, then James Selvin. They let me play basketball with them and treated me like a kid brother.

Brother Dub did all the cooking at the cabin. He also washed our clothes. Dub would fry cornbread every night and I would eat milk and cornbread until my little six-year-old tummy would be tight as a drum. I'd go to bed and sleep soundly all night long, then get up the next morning to find Dub already up and cooking on a pot-bellied stove. This was not a cookstove, but a pot-bellied heater. It was all we had to cook on in the cabin. Dub would make flour batter, drop it into a big, black skillet, let it sizzle and fry, then make a skillet full of sawmill gravy. I would pour that gravy over those fried biscuits and eat three or four of them, drink a large glass of fresh cow's milk, and be ready for a full day in the woods to play.

To brush our teeth, we used a branch from a blackjack tree for a brush and baking soda for toothpaste. That blackjack branch and baking soda really kept your teeth white, and your breath never smelled bad. It didn't taste too good, but it did the trick.

I started to like this place. It was not nearly as pretty as the Choctaw area, but it was a beautiful place. I stopped school again when we moved there, so I was almost seven when I started back to school the following fall.

The first two months we were there, it was very cold. Then, the trees started to get green, and early in the morning the birds would start singing. I got up early in the morning to listen to all types of birds while Dub was cooking. I could not wait to get outside and see what the world was made of. This must have been around March or April. The log cabin was an entirely new place, and I had a lot of looking around and exploring to do in these woods.

We continued to get the *Grit* newspaper monthly, and Dad dutifully read it to keep us informed about world affairs. There were stories about riots in Poland, Germany taking over Austria, and a blind person using what they called a "seeing-eye dog".

"Mister Thornton Wilder won a Pulitzer Prize for that *Our Town* play."

"What's a pullet surprise?"

"It's a big award people get for writin' somethin' real good," said Dub. "Joe Abb, ain't you learned nothin' in school?"

"Well, of course, but we never talked about no pullet surprises." It would be years before I found out the award didn't involve chickens.

On Sundays, Dad would make us go to Sunday school and church. We went to a little wooden Baptist church in Pittsboro. It was about a mile and a half down the road, and we walked there. I'd never attended church regularly before living with Dad, but I remembered the older boys at the orphans' home going, and I thought it was a big deal. I really enjoyed singing the hymns. Sometimes, even the preacher's sermon was interesting. All my school friends went to church there, so it was enjoyable for me.

Very few people had nice clothes in the country, so men and boys wore bib overalls to church, too. They'd put on a white shirt underneath the overalls, and some even had ties. I had some kind of old tie with a rabbit on it. Somebody had tied it for me, and I'd slip it over my neck and tighten up the knot. A few people would wear khaki pants and white shirts to church, but nobody had a suit.

Dad had a bad hip, so he wouldn't go with us to church, but he made us walk there every Sunday. Before we went, he'd take out his money bag and give us each a penny to put in the collection plate. Dad kept his money in an old tobacco sack, tucked into the front of his overalls. Everybody who'd lived through the bank failures during the Depression was mistrustful of banks, and most people kept their money somewhere on them, or hidden around the house. He'd undo the safety pin holding the bag in place, pull it out of the pocket from where he'd tied it to the front of his overalls, undo the drawstring and pull out two pennies for me and Dub. "Now, ya'll put this in during the offering when they pass the plate, you hear?"

"Yessuh."

We'd head off walking down the road to Sunday school, and when they'd pass the collection plate in church, Dub would faithfully put in his penny, every week. I had other plans for mine, though. For a penny, you could get a box of six chocolate kisses. On the way home, I'd stop and buy myself one. "You want a choc'late, Dub?" I'd ask.

"Naw. That's the Lord's money you're spendin' on choc'late, Joe Abb," he'd say. "The devil's gon' get you for that! You gon' have to pay for it one day. You just wait and see."

I'd walk on down the road toward the cabin, happily munching on my chocolates. Dub never did tell our dad about my little transgressions with the candy, even though he wouldn't eat any himself.

Our dad and Dub started clearing land around the log cabin to plant crops. All the large pine trees had been cleared by the sawmill, so they cleared the small bushes. They worked very hard, and it didn't take long before they had about two or three acres cleared.

I didn't know it, but we were about to get some help, and round out our family at the same time. The time had come for John to come home to us.

60

Chapter 15
Lazy Days

My middle brother, John, was still living in the orphan's home in Jackson. Sometimes, he'd stay with a wealthy lady for months, then go back to the home. She lived there in Jackson.

Late one afternoon, the sheriff of Calhoun County drove up. He'd been to Jackson to take some prisoners down there, and my dad had asked him to pick up John and bring him home. As soon as the sheriff's car stopped, my brother got out.

John must have been around eight years old at this time. Even though I hadn't seen him in about three years, I recognized him right away. We stood and looked at each other like a couple of dummies. Dub looked at John, dressed in a suit, and said, "He ain't been up in this part of the woods–he needs to get broke in!"

We behaved until the sheriff left, then got John to change his clothes and we headed out in the woods until suppertime. That night, John slept with Dad on the bed, while Dub and I slept together on the floor.

Somebody gave us an old bed frame, and some lady made us what we called a "bed tick." It wasn't really a mattress, but it was used as one. It was more like a big sock with some sort of a hole in the middle. It was made of heavy material, like canvas, and was the same size as the bed frame. The bed tick was nothing more than a big sack of some sort with a slit in the middle. We all went out into the area where there were no trees and you could find a type of really soft grass, growing very thick. We would pull the grass with our hands, then spread it on the ground so the sun would cure it out. In about a week, it would be cured and we would stuff it in the bed tick, which made us a mattress. We put it on top of the bed slats, which were just plain wood.

It was time to plow the field cleared by Dad and Dub, so he sent the three of us boys over to borrow a mule from a man named Peachtree Smith. We went over to Mr. Smith's place to get the mule, and on the way home we got tired of walking and decided we'd all three try to ride the mule. We'd been told not to do that, but we were tired. Things went fine until we started up that steep hill just down the road from our house. The incline was so steep, I started to slip off the back of the mule.

"Whoa!" I said, as I grabbed at John's overalls in front of me.

John started to slip off right on top of me, and grabbed Dub's overalls in front. All three of us slid right off the back of that mule, which kept on walking, leaving us behind in the dirt. We had to pick ourselves up, run to catch up with the mule and regain control. We walked the rest of the way home, leading the mule behind us. After plowing the field with her the next day, we kept her overnight, then returned her to Mr. Peachtree Smith. We would borrow his mule twice a year to plow our fields.

Every Sunday, Dad still made us go to the local Baptist church. We each had one set of good clothes to wear to church, white pants and a shirt. John wasn't used to going to church there, and I guess he associated it with being in the orphans' home. One week, the Sunday school teacher was trying to teach us how to pray. She said a little prayer, then she went around the circle and had each one of us say a little prayer. I said mine, just like the other children had. Something simple, like "Thank you, God, for everything you give us."

When she came to John, she said, "It's your turn now, John."

He didn't say anything. John always was a little timid. When Dad would make us sing for money, John never wanted to do it.

She repeated, "John? It's your turn to pray, honey."

John just grunted.

She finally decided that he wasn't going to pray and moved on to the next child.

On the walk home, John and I were lagging behind Dub a little. John started making fun of me for praying in Sunday school. "Thaaank yew, Gawwwwd," he said.

"Quit it, John!" I said as I hit him.

It happened to be dewberry season, and John found a bush by the side of the road. I couldn't let him throw those things at me without fighting back, so we got in a huge dewberry fight. That juice got all over our good, white church pants.

"John! Joe Abb! Lawda mercy, the devil's gon' get you both for that!" said Dub when he heard the commotion. The devil may not have gotten us, but boy, Dad was hopping mad when he saw us. I don't think he ever got those dewberry stains out of our pants. It was back to wearing overalls to church for us.

When we harvested the fruits and vegetables from the truck farm, it was more than we could eat. Dad had learned in his youth how to dry vegetables. We didn't have the right kind of jars to can them. He had some long tables out back, and he'd lay the fruits and vegetables out so they'd dry naturally in the sun. For apples, he'd core and slice them. We kept the dried apples in a big box. Dub would stew them with some sugar in a pot, and they tasted just like fresh apples. Dad also dried beans and other things the same way.

John stayed with us for the whole summer, and we went running through the woods every day, building tree houses and forts. There was a lot of wood left lying around from the old sawmills, and we found nails at old fire sites. The thrill was in building these forts, but once they were done, we'd sometimes sit in them and watch the local wildlife. There were also lots of creeks and waterfalls for us to check. We even built one tree house on an island in the middle of a stream.

By August, it was time for school to start again soon, so Dad got out the Sears & Roebuck catalog. That was the only book we had in the house. We all sat down around the table, and Dad took the old-age pension checks he'd saved up and ordered our new shoes and bib overalls for school. I would get two pair of bib overalls and two shirts each year, new, from Sears & Roebuck. Those would have to last me throughout the school year.

Our order would take a couple of weeks to arrive because it had to come all the way from Memphis, Tennessee, about 125 miles north of where we lived. I would always get excited when I got new clothes for school. Of course, people gave us hand-me-downs, too. Usually, our shoes would wear out by the time spring came around, so we'd just go barefoot for the rest of the year.

The news in *Grit* was getting more and more ominous. One month, Japan declared war on China. The Nazis closed the theology department at Innsbruck University in Austria. Some guy named Mussolini in Italy took away the rights of the country's Jews.

Not everything was bad, though. President Roosevelt opened a bridge between the United States and Canada. Howard Hughes was setting world records for round-the-world flights and making passenger flight more available with his "Yankee Clipper". Hughes wasn't the only one flying— some guy they called "Wrong Way Corrigan" landed in Ireland after having set off for California the day before.

Grit kept us informed about all these things, but our day-to-day lives didn't change a bit.

Before we knew it, the summer was over. John went back to live with the rich lady in Jackson. The weather was turning cold early, and school finally started.

We lived a little over a mile away from a town called Pittsboro, Mississippi. It was the county seat. It had two stores, one café and a post office. It also had a little jailhouse that was built two-story, so they could hang people. The building had a scaffold built on it where they used to hang criminals. One garage, a grist mill and two churches, a Baptist

63

and a Methodist. The courthouse had burned down and they were using a vacant grocery store for the courthouse. Up on a high hill was a red brick schoolhouse that taught students from the first through the twelfth grade.

I was the leader of the pack at Pittsboro School, and could beat up any kid in my class and the class above me. Having been in the orphan's home in Jackson, I was exposed to being without a mother or father to look out for me for two years. I had learned to cover my own ass. As I started my second-grade year at Pittsboro, I was looking forward to more of the same. We said goodbye to John and got ready for school to start.

Chapter 16
Mother Figure

I may have started school in Bruce for a very short time, but I will always think of Pittsboro as my first school. You had to live a mile or more from the school to ride the school bus; otherwise, you had to walk. We were lucky. We rode the school bus. The goldenrods were in bloom, and we'd pass fields and fields of them on our way to school.

There was no clock in the log cabin. No timepiece at all; no way to tell time. As a result, we had no way to know when the school bus would show up. Our dad was educated, though, and he had an idea. Dad found a crack in the log cabin, where the early morning sun would shine through. We'd stuffed all the other cracks with newspaper and rags to keep the heat inside. He drew a straight line where the sun was shining the minute the school bus appeared, and that was how we timed the school bus. If it was a cloudy day, one of us would stand outside and listen. You could always hear the engine laboring as the bus came up that steep hill.

Our school bus was just a ton-and-a-half truck. The gentleman who drove it must have built the bed on the back. It looked like a chicken coop. There were wooden benches on both sides and down the middle. All the school buses looked homemade like this.

The school had electric lights, but heat came from large coal-burning stoves, one in each classroom. There was one water pipe in front of the school, and if you wanted a drink you had to go there. Toilets were also outside. If you were facing the front of the school, the boys' outside john was on your right in the woods, and the girls' was to the left.

The teachers in our school were great. Those who finished high school there got a good education. I loved going to school at Pittsboro because there were lots of children to play with. I was not smarter than the others in my class, but I was "street smart". There was a basketball team at the school, but no gym. Both girls and boys played on a clay court. We boys would fight every day, but at the end of the school day, we were best of friends. The only things we had to do were shoot marbles and fight.

When I started the second grade, I had no idea I'd find my first real mother figure. My teacher's name was Ethel Young. She was in her mid-twenties. I walked into that school room and saw the prettiest lady I'd ever seen. She had black hair that hung down below her collar, and she wore makeup and red lipstick. Mrs. Young dressed more modern than the other teachers, more flamboyantly in my eyes. Her husband was a circuit court supervisor who was older than she was. I will always remember her soft, sweet voice.

Living with my dad and two brothers in the log cabin, with no mother and no womenfolk around, Mrs. Young, in my mind, became my mother. I so wanted her to be my mother that I did everything to make her like me. She realized early on my situation, and took pity on me. She would give me clothes, paper to write on, pencils and all my other school supplies. Whenever we'd do a play, she'd give me the lead part. I suppose I really was talented; Dad used to put us on the street corners to sing for money, but this was my first exposure to really performing on a stage, and I loved it.

One December day, when playing out in the woods, I stepped on an old, rusty nail. The thing went into my big toe. I pulled it out and limped back to the log cabin. My father was sitting out on the front porch when I arrived. "What happened to you, son?" said Dad.

"A nail went through my toe!" I whimpered.

"Well, let's have a look at that." He held up my bloody foot and said, "I think we got just the thing to take care of that. Come on over here."

He took me out back and washed my foot with Octagon soap. That was what we used for everything, from washing our feet to laundry, to the dishes. The little yellow octagon-shaped bars had the letters "P&G" carved into them when they were new. We always said that stood for "Push & Grunt" because that's what everybody did at the washboard with it when they were washing clothes.

After washing the wound, Dad got out a chaw of tobacco and chewed it up a little, then put it on my toe and wrapped it up with an old rag. "There," he said, "that'll pull that poison out of there."

My toe still hurt like the dickens, and it swelled up twice as big as the other one. I was able to get my shoe on the next day for school, but my toe hurt so bad, I started crying in class. "Joe Abb, what's the matter?" said Mrs. Young.

"Oh, Miz Young," I said through my tears, "it's my toe. See?" I took off my shoe and held up my foot with its red, swollen digit. She nearly fainted.

"My goodness, Joe Abb, we've got to get something done about that! Lisa, you monitor the class while I go down to the office for a minute. I'll be right back."

Mrs. Young rushed out the door and disappeared for what seemed like forever. When she came back, another teacher was with her. "Class, Miz

Williams is going to take over teaching y'all for the rest of the day. Joe Abb, you come with me."

We went outside to Mrs. Young's car. "Can you walk all right, Joe Abb?"

"Yes'm. I can make it."

"Here, lean on me." She drove me to Bruce, where all the stores had Christmas trees with blinking lights. I was fascinated by that, because we never had a Christmas tree at our house. It almost took my mind off the throbbing pain in my toe. We pulled up in front of the town doctor's office. "Now, Joe, we're goin' to get your toe taken care of here."

"But, Miz Young, I don't have any money to pay for the doctor," I protested.

"Don't you worry about that, young man," she said. "Everything will be fine. Now, come on."

The doctor cleaned up my toe, which was starting to get infected. When he lanced it, pus ran out all over the place. He gave me some kind of a shot and some medicine to put on it. "Now, Joe Abb, you wash your feet and put a dab of this ointment on there every day, you hear?" he told me. Everybody knew everybody in that town, so he was aware that Mrs. Young was not really my mother, no matter how much I wanted her to be.

"Yessuh," I said. My toe didn't hurt any more, and I could get back to playing and fighting, just like always.

Mrs. Young took me across the town square to the general store and bought me some candy. That was a real treat. Then she put her arms around me and said, "Joe Abb, you're a good boy who hasn't had much of a chance in life. I love you and I want to help you however I can."

She drove me back to Pittsboro, then down that old road to the log cabin. I got as close to Mrs. Young as I could, and she let me cuddle up really close. I fell asleep on the drive there. It was well into the darkness when I got home.

Shortly after this, Mrs. Young returned to the log cabin. It was very cold that day, so I was inside instead of out playing in the woods. I ran out to meet the car. "Miz Young! What you doin' here? It sure is good to see you. Come on inside, where it's warm."

"Hey, Joe Abb. I brought you something. Can you help me get these boxes out of the back seat?"

We got the boxes out together and carried them inside. "Dad! Dub! Looky here what Miz Young brung me!"

"*Brought* me," she corrected.

I opened the first box and found it full of clothes. The others were, too. I don't know where she got them, but Dub and I sure did need them. I kept pulling out those used clothes and looking at them like they were the best garments ever made.

The pot-bellied stove was red hot. I noticed Mrs. Young looking around. God only knows what she was thinking. We had toe sacks spread all over the floor to keep the wind from blowing up through the cracks in the floor.

"Here, Miz Young, set here on my nail cag," I offered. We had no chairs, only nail cags to sit on.

"Thank you, Joe Abb," she said, ever gracious. She sat down.

I got as close to her as I could. If she changed position, I'd move up right against her. I was not going to let her get too far away. "Why don't you try on some of the clothes, to see if they fit?" she suggested.

"Okay. You'll wait while I do, right?"

"Oh, yes."

I took a box and headed for the next room to change. Dub came with me, while Dad sat on his nail cag and made small talk with her.

"Awful nice of you to bring those clothes to the boys," he said, in his most educated manner. He always was a charmer.

"Well, it's the least I could do. I know the boys can use them," she said.

I modeled a few outfits for her, and she oohed and aahed over each one. Finally, she announced, "Oh, goodness, look at the time! I've got to get home. Billy will be wanting his supper."

I followed her to the car. She put her arms around me and hugged me really tight. I would not let her go. She finally had to pull my little hands away from her. "Now, Joe Abb, I'll see you Monday in school, okay?"

"Yez'm, Miz Young," I said. She was the first person I'd ever gotten a lump in my throat for. In the two years she was my teacher, Mrs. Young always looked out for me and made sure we got something for Christmas.

One day around Christmastime, Dub and I were outside in the front garden when a car came by on the road. As it passed, it threw something out the window. "What was that, Dub?"

"I don't know. Let's go see."

We went down to the roadside and picked up a piece of paper that had a picture of a man and woman who looked like they were about to kiss on the top of it. At the bottom, it said "GONE WITH THE WIND". Dub and I looked it over, then looked at each other.

"What's Gone With the Wind, Dub?"

"I don't know, Joe Abb, but *somethin's* gone with the wind." We both laughed and went back to playing in the front garden.

As the cold winter passed, the birds and wildlife started moving about. Leaves came out and everything turned green. There were all kinds of wild flowers growing throughout the woods. The morning glories would just grow wild. Dogwood trees, both white and pink ones, dotted the landscape. It was the perfect place for a tough boy to grow up.

"What's in the *Grit* this month?" I asked upon arriving home one afternoon to find Dad sitting on the front porch, reading the newspaper.

"Well, let's see...President Roosevelt's tryin' to get Social Security checks for women and children."

"I thought Social Security was for old people, when they retired."

"Yeah, I think when it started it was, but he's changing that. And now we're selling war planes to France."

"How come?"

"Well, those Nazis in Germany are on the rampage, and they're starting to threaten some of the other European countries. Now they've launched this new battleship. They call it the *Bismarck.*"

"What if they start coming over here?"

"That's what everybody's worried about. If this Hitler takes over Europe, who's to say that'll satisfy him?"

I thought about my beautiful woods, all my tree houses, and my life here. That was the last thing I wanted, for any of it to change.

My dad started planting his truck farm. There was always a peanut patch, corn, strawberries, and a big garden for our vegetables. I was still too young to work the truck farm, so I was free to roam the woods when I was not in school. I spent my springs this way for two years, blissful and fulfilled. The thought of my mother was always in the back of my mind, and I kept thinking that she would appear in front of me again someday. But as time went on, and we got busier with the farm, I thought less and less about her. Could things get any better? They were about to.

Chapter 17
Boy's Best Friend

Spring was here, and the weather was starting to get warm. This spring and summer, however, would be different from those in my past.

I was visiting with the Easley family down the road one day when Mr. Jim Easley called me outside. "Joe Abb, I got somethin' for you," he said, holding a whimpering, squirming little bundle of white, tan and black in his hands.

"A puppy? For me, suh?" I said, taking it from him. The little Feist dog squealed and cried in my arms, then started licking my face.

"Yep, he's all yours. Now, you'll take good care of him, won't you?"

"Yessuh!" I said.

"What you gon' name him, Joe Abb?" asked James Selvin.

"Well, since your daddy gave him to me, I think I'll call him Jimbo."

"Got somethin' else for you, too," said Mr. Easley.

"Holy smokes!" said James Selvin. "What could be better'n a dawg? It ain't his birthday, or nothin'!"

Mr. Easley reached into the pocket of his trousers and gave me a pocket knife. The handle was a brown, plastic material we called citaloid. Although small and lightweight, the two blades were made of solid steel. Now, this was something special. Every man carried a pocket knife on him. Getting one of my own was sort of a rite of passage. My eyes were as big as saucers.

"A pocket knife of my very own? Gee, thanks, Mister Easley!"

"You're welcome. You know how to open it?"

"Yessuh! I seen my daddy do it a hundred times!" Using my thumbnail, I easily opened the big blade of the knife, but had a hard time getting my little fingers in it to open the smaller blade. It was a perfect knife for a boy my age.

"Alright. Now, you be careful with that, boy," he said. "Don't get excited and be cutting anybody with it. You just use it out in the woods, like a young boy should."

"Yessuh," I said, my eyes never leaving the instrument. I put it in my pocket and walked a little taller on the way home.

"Dad! Dub! Look what Mister Jim Easley gave me," I yelled as I walked in the log cabin.

"Boy! Get that dog outta this house!" said Dad.

"Yessuh. Ain't he cute, Dad?"

Jimbo looked up at my father from my arms, like he was asking if he could stay.

"What's his name?" asked Dub.

"Jimbo, after Mister Jim Easley," I said.

"Jimbo, huh? Well, li'l feller, I reckon you're a part of the family now," said Dad, scratching the puppy behind the ears. "But he's gon' sleep outside, you hear?"

"Yessuh. Oh, and I almost forgot. Look what else he gave me." I pulled the knife out of my pocket and held it out to my dad.

"Uh-huh. That's a nice little pocket knife, right there," he said. "Did you tell him thank you?"

"Yessuh."

"Make sure you take good care of that, and don't be throwing it at anybody, you hear?"

"Yessuh."

"Tonight I'll show you how to sharpen it."

"Awright, suh."

"And take that dog outside."

"Yessuh." Jimbo and I headed out back to the woods.

Jimbo became my constant companion. We'd walk through the woods together and he'd always let me know if there were any snakes ahead of us. There were lots of snakes out in those woods. I loved that little dog more than anything.

One day, Jimbo and I were walking down a small creek about three to six inches deep, between two small hills. We happened upon a snake lying on the bank of the stream. Jimbo started barking, but the old snake did not move. "That's funny," I said, "for that snake to just lie there like that." It was still alive; I could see it breathing.

While Jimbo was still barking at the snake, I got a large stick and started hitting it. Between Jimbo and me, we killed the thing. Finding a forked stick on the ground, I held it over the snake's head so it wouldn't bite me, just in case there was still some life left in it.

After looking over the snake, I found that it had a huge lump in its midsection. "What on earth could that be?" I said to Jimbo. He seemed as puzzled as I was. I took out my pocket knife and cut the snake open. Out crawled a little baby turtle! Lo and behold, it was still alive. The little turtle crawled away and the mean old snake died. Just a normal day with a boy and his dog out in the woods in the 1930's, in the great state of

Mississippi.

The weather got warmer and I noticed on the side of Sand Hill, down the road about an eighth of a mile, were all kinds of grapes. We called them "possum grapes." They were hard to get because the vines would grow from the ground up to the outward part of a tree limb, and if you went too far out on the limb, it would break off. Sometimes you could find a good, strong limb, crawl out on it and eat grapes for hours. But the next day, your tummy would send you running to the outside john! With me, I never knew when to stop eating those good, sweet possum grapes.

There were also dewberries all over the woods, and huckleberries. The kind we called huckleberries grew from a crooked tree or a bush. You could climb the huckleberry bush very easily, sit up in it and eat the little huckleberries.

One day I came home with a bucketful of those sweet possum grapes and Dub said, "You know what our mother used those for?"

"Naw, Dub," I said. "What?"

"She made wine out of 'em."

"What's wine?"

"I swear, Joe Abb, you don't know nothin'! It's somethin' the grownups drink. Makes 'em giggle and act silly."

"Grownups drink it, huh? How do you make it?"

"Well, first you gotta get the juice outta the grapes," he said, then explained to me the whole process how our mother had made wine from possum grapes. Dub had been with her for most of his life, and he paid very close attention to everything she did, so he knew every detail.

The next day, I went back to Sand Hill and got more grapes. I took along some sugar that we had gotten from the welfare. I made myself about a gallon of good, strong wine, just the way Dub had told me our mother used to make it. It was good grape wine. The road where I'd found the grapes and made the wine was never used any more; it dated from the time of the Civil War. Trees grew out of the middle of it, but you could still tell there was a road there. Sometimes you'd see the big, heavy banks on the side and know it had been there, but it wasn't really a road any more. This was where I decided to hide my jug of wine. I dug a hole next to the old road and buried the container, then went home and forgot all about it.

"Dad, you look worried. What's wrong?" I had just come in from my daily jaunt through the woods.

"Things don't look good in Europe, Joe Abb," he said.

"Oh, you must've gotten the *Grit* today."

"Yes. They've cancelled the Olympic Games for this year because of the war in Europe."

72

"I didn't think you ever followed sports, Dad."

"Usually, I don't, but this is more than just about sports. The Nazis have taken over Holland now, and they're moving into France. England has a new prime minister, though, and he seems to be more willing to stand up to that Hitler."

"What's his name?"

"A Mister Churchill."

"Well, with a name like that, he oughta be a God-fearin' man, right?"

"Yeah, Joe Abb, I guess." His brow remained furrowed, though, and my weak attempt at humor didn't seem to relieve his concern any.

Chapter 18
Summer Mischief

When summer arrived, John returned to us from the rich lady's in Jackson. It was good to see him again. He was almost getting old enough to help Dad and Dub out with the truck farm, but still found some time to spend with me and my friends.

That summer, I spent most of the time playing with a couple of boys who lived about a mile away. One's name was L.T. Cleveland. Half the kids then were known by their initials, or for some, that was just their names. I only ever knew this boy as L.T. he was about thirteen years old, and I was still eight. L.T. was a hefty boy with brown hair, and he always played with boys younger than himself. He chewed tobacco and dipped snuff, just like the grown men.

My other friend from that summer was Sam Parker. About my age, and from a good family, Sam always looked neat. He had dark hair, and was about average height for a boy our age. Sam was the only boy in the family, with three sisters. He was funny and athletic.

L.T., Sam, John and I would team up and go swimming in a cow pond. That was a pond that was dammed up so the water would gather there for the cattle to drink during times of drought. All the young boys would find out where these were, and that's where we'd do our swimming. We called this one Kilgore Pond. The four of us would head about half a mile through the woods and swim half the day in that old, muddy cow pond. Jimbo always came along, too.

On the way back home, we would stop by Mr. Raleigh's watermelon patch and take one of his watermelons. I was the youngest, so I was the one who had to sneak into the field to get the melon. You could see Mr. Raleigh's house from the watermelon patch.

One day, I was getting a very large watermelon, crawling on my belly and pushing it in front of me, trying to stay low so Mr. Raleigh could not see me. Suddenly, I heard this loud voice yelling, "Joe Abb Overby! Them watermelons is poison! I'm tellin' you again, you little son-of-a-gun, them watermelons is poison! You son-of-a-gun, you best leave 'em alone!"

It was a lady's voice; sounded like one of Mr. Raleigh's daughters. I was so close to the ground, I could not believe she could see me. Sam, L.T.

and John were saying, "Hurry, before we all get caught! Get this damn watermelon outta here so we can haul ass outta this place! Soon as we get it out in the woods, we gon' sit down and eat us some watermelon." Jimbo was barking at her for yelling at me. He was always very protective of me.

"Jimbo! Quiet, boy!" I told him. "We gon' get caught!" He always seemed to understand me when I told him things like this, and immediately stopped barking.

Seemed like I was always the one to do the dirty work. We knew where every hay-shakin' farmer's watermelon patch was within two miles of this place. If it wasn't Mr. Raleigh's patch, it was somebody else's. It seemed the summer would never end. L.T. kept Sam and me in hot water all the time, but I didn't always need his help to get there.

Later in the summer, I was walking along the old Civil War road and remembered that jug of wine I'd made a couple months earlier. I was able to find the place where I'd buried it without much trouble. After digging it up and wiping the dirt off it around the top, I started sipping the wine I had made.

Boy, did it taste good! It was really good and sweet. So good, in fact, I kept on drinking it, and even poured some into the lid of that Mason jar for Jimbo to drink. Altogether, I probably drank about a tall water glassful. When I had my fill, I buried the wine jug in my "hideaway" again. About half an hour later, I started feeling dizzy. Jimbo was acting kind of funny, too. We started staggering back through the woods, toward the log cabin. At one point, I got so dizzy, I had to lie down on the ground. I fell asleep for a while.

When Jimbo and I got back to the log cabin, I told Dub I was sick.

"What's wrong?" he said.

"Well, remember how you told me how our momma used to make that wine?"

"Yeah."

"Well, I made me some, and when I was just out in the woods, I remembered about it, so I dug it up an' drunk me a li'l bit."

"Lawdy, Joe, the devil is surely gon' get you! You need to go to bed, right now," he said.

"Without even washin' my feet?"

"Yep. Now, go get in the bed. I Sewanee, the devil is gon' get you, boy."

I crawled into bed. It really did feel good, and I was still a little dizzy. I slept all night without waking up.

Next day, my dad called me out back, where he was holding a little switch cut off one of his peach trees. "I hear you been drinkin' wine, boy," he said.

"Yessuh." I had felt all grown up, but the sight of that switch was bringing me back to reality.

Dad proceeded to spank the heck out of me with that peach switch. When he was finished, he sat me down in a cane-bottomed chair out in the yard and talked to me for about half an hour.

"Where'd you get that wine?"

"Made it myself, with some ol' possum grapes out in the woods."

He shook his head and looked at the ground. "Boy, if you ever, *if you ever* live to be twenty-one years old, you gon' wind up in the state penitentiary."

"Yessuh."

"You don't wanna go to no state penitentiary."

"Naw suh." I figured he knew whereof he spoke.

"I had better not catch you doin' that, ever again, you hear me?"

"Yessuh."

He must have scared me to death, because I never did go back for the rest of that wine.

The Baptist church in Pittsboro had built what they called an "oak arbor" in the woods. They made it by clearing the underbrush around some big oak trees, then they cut several of the limbs off so they could hang lanterns around the clearing. Those lanterns would really light up the place. They made benches our of old sawmill strips, and even built a little pulpit.

The oak arbor was a lot closer to our cabin than the church itself, and our dad would go there some evenings with us for their services. One lady would just yell and beat her fan on one of the trees during one part of the service when they were singing. I would think, "That woman's crazy!" There was no store between the oak arbor and the cabin, so my little candy scam was no more once we started going to church there. I would probably never have been able to pull it off, anyway, when Dad went there with us.

Where the oak arbor was located eventually became a bona fide church called Oak Grove. I even went there in the early 1990s for its 50th anniversary.

Like a lot of men at the time, my dad would chew tobacco, dip snuff and smoke cigars. When he would get his old-age pension check every month, he would buy a handful of cigars. They cost five cents apiece. You could get two for five cents, but those were much smaller than the ones my dad liked. He would keep his cigars behind a rubber band inside a grip on a shelf, stored neatly in a straight line. Every night, he would smoke half a cigar, then put the other half back behind the rubber band for the next night.

We would all sit around in the evenings out on a little porch he'd built. Dub and I would always wash our feet there before we went to bed. We never took a bath, just washed our hands, faces and feet with Octagon P&G soap in a small pan before bedtime. Dad would buy one of the yellow bars of Octagon, and it would last us for a whole month. We used it for washing ourselves, as well as the dishes; it worked for everything.

We had no electricity. There was a coal oil lamp, but we didn't use it for anything except to study school homework. Most of our work was done before the sun went down. Almost every night, we would sit out there and sing, usually the same old songs, over and over. *Maple on the Hill, Get Along Home, Cindy*, and others.

Around noon one day, I looked down the road and saw L.T. coming toward me with his overalls on, no shirt. I was dressed the same. That was all we had to wear. Shoes were only for in the wintertime.

I was always glad to see L.T. I looked up to him, but he usually got me into trouble. He really was not a bad boy, but always played with younger boys and led us down the wrong road. I could tell he had something big on his mind.

He said, "Joe Abb, I got us a big deal!"

Boy, I was ready to participate in this big deal. As we were going out to the cow pond for our swim, he said, "I saw your dad's cigars up on that shelf yesterday." He said the word "cigars" with the accent on the first syllable. "They's them big five-cent cigars. I was in Mister Wooten's store in Pittsboro, and I took a handful of them two-for-five-cent cigars when he wasn't lookin'. So here's what I want you to do."

"Yeah. I'm listenin'."

"I want you to take them big five-cent cigars and swap 'em out for these little ones. Your dad will never know the difference. Then we'll haul ass to the swimmin' hole."

Why I believed my dad would never notice the difference, I don't know, but L.T. was very convincing. He was 13, after all, and I was only 8. I exchanged the cigars. Any fool could tell the difference between the two. But L.T. and I smoked those big cigars like we were big shots. They made me sick, sicker than that wine I'd made from the possum grapes. But L.T. seemed to really enjoy them.

That night, my dad went to get his evening cigar. Of course, it was dark in the cabin. He put the cigar in his mouth and lit it up. Then he said to Dub, "Something's wrong with this cigar."

He took the coal-oil lamp, struck a match and lit it. Then he looked at the cigar and said, "That damn Wooten put these cheap cigars in my bag and charged me for the big ones! I think he must have some Jew blood in him."

The next day, my dad walked all the way to Mr. Wooten's store, and I went with him. He showed the cigars to Mr. Wooten and said, "You know I always buy those big cigars. You *know* that!"

Mr. Wooten said, "Mister Bill, I *gave* you the big cigars."

"Well, then how did I wind up with all these little cigars?" He showed Mr. Wooten that handful of little smokes.

Mr. Wooten looked puzzled, shook his head and examined the cigars. He said, "I can't understand what to hell is goin' on any more."

I was standing there, watching the whole show, not blinking an eye. I was scared to death during the whole conversation. Mr. Wooten swapped out the cigars for my dad, and thought he'd made the mistake. "I'm sorry about that, Mister Bill. Next time you come in, make sure I give you the right ones."

"Damn sure will; I ain't gonna get gypped again!"

As we started to leave the store, Mr. Wooten looked at me and said, "Here's a piece of candy for you, son. You seem to be the only person standin' here knows what to hell is actually goin' on."

Taking the candy, I said, "Thanks, Mister Wooten."

We headed back down the old country road to the cabin.

That was about the last time I ever saw L.T. Sam and I stayed together for a while after that, and still see each other at the school reunion every two years.

Chapter 19
Last Hurrah

By Halloween, the leaves on the maples were turning brilliant reds and golds. We didn't have an outside john at the log cabin, so when the weather got cold, we learned to go quickly.

In the cold months, one of our pastimes was to sit in the cabin around the old pot-bellied stove with a fire. Sometimes it would be red-hot, other times not so. We would pop popcorn on the stove. My dad would sometimes parch regular corn. I never understood this, but I guess with his being so old, back in his days they would parch regular corn—put it in a skillet and heat it up with some lard until it would crack open. I sometimes would eat this cracked corn with my dad. You had to have good teeth to do this.

Dub would pop the popcorn, then pour sorghum molasses over it and make it into balls. Putting some sugar in the molasses made them a little sweeter. To me, that was great. Eating popcorn balls was just like eating a piece of store-bought candy.

Of course, we also had parched peanuts that my dad had grown. After eating all of that, with a tummy full, I would go to bed and snuggle up to my older brother, Dub. Before I went to sleep, I would look out the small section of the window—there were only two windows in the whole log cabin—and see a golden moon and wonder what was on that beautiful, round object. Somehow, I just could not believe that it was made of cheese, like the boys at school said.

Some nights, we'd go down the road to the Easleys' house. They had a radio. It was a big thing, with a huge battery underneath it. The first thing I ever heard on the radio was a fight between Joe Lewis and Billy Kahn. Boy, that was something! The Easleys would only use the radio to listen to certain shows, like the Grand Ole Opry on Saturday nights. We all loved that show. When the battery under the radio was getting low, the sound would fade in and out.

At Christmas time, Dad actually had enough money this year to buy us each a present. John and I each got a sack of marbles and Dub got some firecrackers. We still got our stockings from the welfare with an apple and an orange in them. I also got a bag of switches—little peach switches, all cut into the same length—with a note from Santa telling me to shape

79

up. I found out later that John and Dub had done that. We didn't have a Christmas tree in the cabin, but there was one at school. We all helped decorate it by making ornaments out of tinfoil.

The *Grit* newspaper continued to bring us gloom and doom about the war in Europe. The Germans were bombing London, and British troops were marching into northern Africa. "We're going to end up fightin' in this war, yet," Dad would say.

He was almost as distraught at the deaths of authors F. Scott Fitzgerald and James Joyce, just a few weeks apart. "Boys, they were two of the greatest writers of this century, one American and one Irish."

"What'd they write?"

"Fitzgerald wrote a book about rich folks back in the '20s. First time I ever read that book, it was like I was taken into a whole different world. It was nothin' like I ever knew here in Mississippi. Joyce was from a working family in Ireland, and he wrote about that. But, outside of the settings, they both wrote about the most basic human feelings and actions. Yep, people are the same everywhere, no matter how much money they got or where they live. You boys'll get to read some of those books later on in school."

Winter passed and the spring sprung. We started the garden and the truck farm all over again. It just could not get any better. The same routine every year. This was my fourth spring there, and I had turned nine years old in the fall.

Other boys and girls at school had nice clothes to wear, but I kept wearing the same old ones with holes in them. As young as I was, I never really paid attention to clothes and things like that. But now, we were getting older. I had started paying attention and noticing that we were behind in society. I was starting to look down on myself as being a very poor boy.

One morning, we were having breakfast around the wooden table at the cabin. Biscuits and thickening gravy, fatback and hog meat. That was all we had. My dad was saying grace, and he just started crying. I looked at Dub and he did not know any more than I what to do. Dad went outside while Dub and I finished eating, then we caught the bus and went to school. This would be my last year of school at Pittsboro.

We continued on with school and things stayed about the same around the old cabin. John came back to us in the summer. He and I were full of mean little things to do. We dreamed up a prank to pull on our dad.

Behind the cabin was a tree that had blown down during a windstorm, and it was used as an outside john. You could climb up the tree at a very low angle, hold onto another limb and do number two. My dad had corn cobs stacked up on a forked limb of the tree, to clean himself after doing his number two. We kids were forbidden from using these corn cobs; they were strictly for him.

John and I took the corn cobs and went out to the garden. Dad had been growing some hot peppers there, so we took some and rubbed the cobs really good with them. We even cut open the hot peppers and rubbed them until all the juice was on the corn cobs. Then we took the cobs back to the angled, blown-down tree and put them back where he kept them.

Later in the evening, we saw our dad heading for the outside john and we knew what he was going to do. We hid in the bushes where we could see him the whole time. When he finished, he reached for the corn cobs and cleaned himself real good using five or six of them. Then he crawled down from the angled tree and started walking away.

Suddenly, he stopped, then started again. Stopped, then started again. Scratched his ass, took some short leaps and started running ninety miles an hour to a little creek about two hundred feet away. He was screaming and trying to sing at the same time. It looked as though he had lost his mind. He took his overalls off, jumped into the water and started washing his behind with all the strength he had.

This lasted for about ten to fifteen minutes. Then he got out of the creek, picked up his overalls and started walking down the path to the old log cabin. We came out of the bushes as though we were just walking through the woods, trying to stop laughing. I said, "Dad, I heard you screamin'. Is there somethin' wrong?"

"No, I think some damn skunk or wildcat must've pissed on my corn cobs. It burnt my butt so bad, I could hardly stand it."

He never dreamed we boys had anything to do with this whole thing, and never did find out the truth.

Dad walked in one day looking sad. "Boys, I have some sad news," he said.

"What is it, Dad?" Dub and I gathered around him.

"Mister Raleigh has died." Nobody I'd ever known had died yet, so this was a new thing for me.

"When's his funeral gon' be?" asked Dub.

"In a few days. He's gon' be embalmed."

"What's embalmed?" I asked.

"That's when they pump all the blood out of your body and pump in this fluid that keeps you from rottin'," explained Dub.

"Oh." It didn't sound too appealing to me. I wondered which would be worse, rotting or being embalmed.

The funeral was to be in the Baptist church. We all wore our usual church-going clothes, pants and a white shirt and a tie. It was my first funeral. We went up to Mister Raleigh's casket, and there he was, looking like a man asleep. But he didn't look quite right. It almost looked like he

81

was made of wax. He was dressed in a suit and tie, which I had never seen him wear before. He had always worn bib overalls, just like the rest of us. It was hard to believe he was dead. I felt kind of bad for stealing so many of his watermelons. Mister Raleigh was somebody I had always liked.

We found a seat and the service started before long. There were some sad songs, and Mrs. Raleigh was crying up on the front row. The songs seemed to make her sadder. Then the preacher said some nice things about Mr. Raleigh, we sang another song, had a prayer, and it was over. The funeral director went over and closed the lid of the casket. Six men went up and carried the casket out of the church. Dad said there was going to be another part of the service at the side of Mr. Raleigh's grave, but we didn't go to that.

The next day, Dad went off somewhere to visit one of his old friends. He left us three boys alone at the cabin. John and I decided to build a parachute from some old clothes and some string that we had in the barn, then take the cat up on top of the log cabin and let him drop slowly to the ground. John came up with the idea, but we both thought this would be fun.

Ol' Tom was a big, fat gray and white cat who had taken up at our house. We fed him some scraps, but he mainly ate birds and whatever else he caught on his own. He liked being around us, and was always underfoot.

We got all the material—clothes, cloth, string, scissors—and put together a parachute. We had no problem catching Tom. When everything was put together, I went behind the corn crib and got the ladder so I could get up on top of the cabin. It was a homemade ladder.

I took the little parachute up first, then came back down to get Ol' Tomcat. He was happy to go up the ladder with me. I got everything over close to the edge of the cabin and tied the parachute to Ol' Tom. John was standing by on the ground.

"Don't drop him, Joe Abb," he instructed me. "Slowly throw him up real high so the parachute will catch more air and he'll float down slower."

By that time, Ol' Tom was getting a little excited and wondering what to hell was going on. I threw him up as high as I could, and that cat let out a cat-scream meow that I'd never heard in all my life, not before or since. At the highest point, he began to urinate, and did so all the way down. He made about fifteen complete flips in mid-air, wrapping that parachute and string around him so tight that when he hit the ground it looked like he was in a straitjacket. It was like a little bundle of shower coming down in the yard.

John ran over to the cat and tried to untangle him from the parachute.

"Ow! Owie!" I heard John yelling from below as the cat yowled and fought him. Ol' Tom scratched the hell out of John, then took off into the woods as soon as he was free. He must not have been hurt. You couldn't say as much for John.

The day was starting to get warmer; it must have been close to noon. I started to go back to the ladder to get off the roof, only to find that John had removed it. There I was, on top of the cabin, and could not get off. John said, "You messed up the parachute so bad, I'm gonna punish you for not makin' it better." He was still nursing his wounds from where Ol' Tom had torn him up.

"Punish me how?"

"By makin' you stay up there 'til the mailman comes by. He usually runs the mail by around noon. By the way, Mister Hanniford is our mailman. You know that, don't you?"

"Yes, I know that."

"Well, I'm gon' tell him you love his daughter and see what he has to say about that!"

Mr. Hanniford's daughter was a girl named Dorothy. She and I were the same age and in the same class at school. Dorothy was the prettiest girl in the class. I had bragged to all the other boys in school that she was my girlfriend and I did not want anybody messing with her, or I would beat them up.

"Please, John, don't stop Mister Hanniford and tell him nothin'!"

"Yessuh, I'm gon' tell him!"

"Aw, come on, John! I didn't mean to make the parachute bad. Let me down, will you?"

It was starting to look like I had no other option than to wait for Mr. Hanniford to shoot me for loving his daughter. He drove a light green Chevrolet car, probably a 1932 model. I didn't know whether to jump off the cabin and break my leg, or wait to get shot, so I just sat there, begging and crying. Finally, brother Dub put the ladder up to the roof again and I came down. I must've looked just like Ol' Tom when I shot into the woods. By the time Mr. Hanniford came by at noon, I was hidden deep in the trees.

We didn't see Ol' Tom for two or three days, then he showed up, meowing for food, just like always. But he didn't come near me for months afterward.

One of the saddest days of my young life was about to happen. John, Dub, Dad and I were walking up Sand Hill to get some muscadines. That was a type of grape that grew on the big trees up there. The hill was quite steep, and there was a sharp curve in the middle of it. There was no house within almost a mile of where we were, just large trees, grapevines, persimmon trees and woods. A car came down the hill pretty fast, then we heard a strange, loud yelp, followed by a long howl behind us. My thought was immediate: Jimbo!

He was some distance behind us, and I just knew he'd been hit by this speeding car. We all ran back down the hill about halfway, and there was Jimbo, lying in the road. His little body was crushed, but his tail was wagging still. More like shaking, really. Blood was coming out of his mouth and his little eyes were kind of flickering. He recognized me and looked up at me, making pitiful whimpering sounds from time to time.

The dust was still hanging in the air from where the car had passed. It never stopped; nobody would have stopped in those days when they hit an animal. I started to cry as my dad picked up Jimbo and said, "Let's throw him off the road."

"Off the road? Why, Dad?"

"'Cause, son, he's gonna be dead in a few minutes. I'm gon' throw him off in the woods so nothing else'll run over him."

I cried and begged, "Please, Dad, don't throw him out in the woods! His little tail's still movin'!"

I lay down on the ground alongside my dog, crying, "Please, please, let me take him back to the cabin. I'll take good care of Jimbo. Please!"

But Dad was pretty rough. He knew the dog would not live, so he picked him up and threw his little body as far as he could off the road, saying, "We can get you another dog."

It was starting to get late, so we turned and went home in silence. There were still chores to be done around the cabin, getting water and stove wood to cook the next day, and all. We ate our supper and went to bed. I lay in bed wondering why God had taken my dog away. He had been with me since he was six weeks old, the first dog I'd ever had. Half the night, I lay awake, thinking about how much Jimbo and I loved each other.

At daybreak the next morning, I got up while everyone else was still sleeping. Going out on the porch, I found a big grub hoe and a shovel. I took them with me, back to Sand Hill, and walked down the side of the road where my dad had thrown Jimbo off in the woods, looking for him. Finally, I saw a spot of white in the green bushes, and there he was. His little body was stiff and unmoving. There was no odor yet, but his face was bloodied pretty badly. Flies were drawn to the blood, and were buzzing around his head. There were always buzzards circling over those woods, whenever something would die in there. I was not going to let the buzzards eat my dog. I was going to wrap him up and give him a nice funeral. As I stood over my dead Jimbo, I began to cry again. No one was there but me.

I dug a deep hole, crying all the time, and put Jimbo in it. It seemed appropriate to sing him a song, so I sang the song I'd heard at Mr. Raleigh's funeral, *The Father Alone Will Know About It*. That was the only funeral I'd ever been to. I could hardly sing for crying.

That fall would be lonely, roaming through the woods and creeks without my buddy, Jimbo. Dad never let me have another dog. As I would go to the spring to fetch water for the next day, late in the evening, I would always stop by to say hello to my dog, Jimbo.

Chapter 20
Changes Coming

On that December day, we were in school at Pittsboro when Mrs. Young was called out into the hallway and came back in the room with all the color run out of her face. "Class...oh, class, it's horrible!" she said, and began sobbing.

We were all looking at each other and wondering what to do. "Miz Young? Don't cry. What's wrong?"

She composed herself and told us the horrible news, about the attack on Pearl Harbor in Hawaii that morning. It was already after lunch, and almost time for us to go home for the day, when the news came. "Let's join together and sing," said Miss Young, regaining her composure. "Joe Abb, will you come up and lead us in *God Bless America*?"

I did, and afterward we continued singing *My Country, 'Tis of Thee* and other patriotic songs. We didn't know what else to do. We were all numb, as was the rest of the country.

The school sent us all home early, and was closed for a week or two. They turned the school into a makeshift recruiting station. All the men and boys who were of age wanted to sign up to fight the "Japs" who had attacked us.

When we finally started back to school, I saw a strange-looking man looking across the schoolyard. He had his arms around a very pretty girl. I ran up as close as I could get to him and said, "Hey, what are you?"

"I'm in the United States Navy!" he replied. He was wearing those bell-bottomed trousers with the thirteen buttons on them, a long blue-and-white collar hanging down his back, and a long scarf around his neck. His shoes were shined like a mirror.

"You sure do have a lot of buttons on your pants."

"Yup. Thirteen, to be exact."

"Why you have thirteen buttons on your pants?"

He laughed and said, "That's to give the girls thirteen chances to say 'no'."

The other boys told me he had graduated from Pittsboro High School the previous year. That encounter sparked a desire in me to join the Navy someday.

During my second-and third-grade years of school, President Roosevelt's welfare project was building us a wooden gymnasium. It was finally finished just after the first of the year, with a soup kitchen on the side of it. I used to eat there sometimes, because we were so poor. That gymnasium was the biggest wooden building I'd ever seen. When we finally went inside, it was heated by two big coal-burning stoves, just like the classrooms, one on each side of the gym. We really thought we had arrived, with that nice, new gymnasium.

Jobs began to come to our county and the adjacent ones. The government built an Army camp down the road at Grenada. Everybody got a job except my dad. He was in his early seventies by now, and was too old for a job. His old-age pension did get raised quite a bit, though, because of the improving economy.

This was the last year that Mrs. Young would be my teacher. She and her husband were about to move away, and I later heard from one of the other boys that she was teaching at another school down in Calhoun County. Mrs. Young was my teacher through the second and third grades at Pittsboro, and I still have a photograph of her. I would always remember the lessons she taught me about how you cannot live without love.

Brother John went back to the rich lady in Jackson, to live with her again. That left Dub and me still in the cabin with our dad. John seemed to always be bouncing back and forth from the cabin to Jackson. I was about to do a little bouncing myself.

Chapter 21
The Next Journey

One spring day, around noon, an old 1932 black Buick came down the gravel road and stopped by our mailbox. Two men and a lady I had never seen before got out, stretched and started walking up the path through the garden to our cabin. One man was small, about in his fifties, with gray hair. The other was about average height, maybe in his mid-thirties, and he combed his black hair straight back with no part. Both the men had on khaki pants and white shirts. The lady was probably in her late twenties. She was tiny and beautiful, with black, curly hair and was wearing a print dress. They were all smiling.

My dad shook hands with the younger man and hugged his neck. "Joe Abb, Dub, come here," he said. "I want you to meet y'all's half-brother, Winfred."

So, this was one of Dad's children from his first marriage. The woman spoke to me first. "You must be Joe Abb. I'm Lilly, Winfred's wife. How do you do?" She seemed very nice, and I liked her immediately.

Winfred introduced the older man to my dad. "This here's Mister Dorman, Lilly's daddy."

"Pleased to meet you, Mister Dorman," said my dad.

"Likewise, Mister Overby."

"I got your letter," continued Winfred. Letter? What letter? I looked over at Dub.

"I'll tell you later," he whispered to me.

The car belonged to Mr. Dorman. He was like a grandfather, a very good man who loved children. He and his wife had twin daughters, Lilly and Willy, but he didn't have any boys of his own. Mr. Dorman took a liking to me right away. He owned a dairy, and sold the milk from it to hospitals.

The visitors stayed with us about four hours. Dad walked them around the truck farm, showing them all the crops. Dub and I trailed along behind the group, just close enough to catch some of the conversation, but far enough away so that we could whisper out of earshot.

"What was he talkin' about, Dad's letter?" I whispered to Dub.

"It was a letter Dad wrote to him about us," he said.

"Us?"

"Yeah, us."

"What *about* us? Why would he write to Winfred about us?"

"'Cause, Joe Abb, Dad's gettin' old. He can't take care of us the way he used to."

"Well, we do all right."

"Yeah, I know, but it's really hard for him. He sent a letter to each one of his three boys from his first wife, askin' them to take one of us boys to live with 'em."

"What?! But we don't even *know* 'em! Hey, how do *you* know about all this, anyway?"

"I helped him write the letters. Now, hush so's we can hear what they're sayin'!"

A lot of their conversation seemed to be centered on me. We decided they must have come to see what I was made of, to satisfy themselves if they wanted to take on the responsibility of raising me.

They finally left, a long trail of dust behind the old black Buick. They never said a word to me about taking me with them, so I figured they had decided not to. I went on with my life, never knowing all that had been discussed and decided that day. Before long, I was off in the woods, checking on my waterfalls and tree houses. I still missed Jimbo, but was beginning to get along without him.

Before we knew it, school was out for the summer, so Sam Parker and I got together to cut stove wood. I'd come up with this big deal for us to cut stove wood. We were going to sell it and get rich. My dad had done something similar when we had first moved to the cabin, and I decided that Sam and I were old enough to get some of that kind of money. We were both ten years old by now.

Most everyone used wood to cook in those days. We all had wooden cook stoves. There was no electricity out on that road. Sam and I would go to the cow pond in the mornings to swim. Then his mother would cook us a good lunch. After that, we'd cut wood for about three hours, sleep for a while, then I would go home for the day. We did this for about a month.

Sam and I were always talking about selling our stove wood and how much money we were going to make from it. We were storing it on Mr. Parker's land until we made this big sales push, I guess to make sure we had enough wood first.

This was not to be, however. One Saturday morning at daybreak, Dad said, "Son, we gon' pack up all your clothes and walk to Bruce."

"Why, Dad?"

"I'm gon' put you on a milk truck, and you are goin' to Pontotoc."

"Pontotoc? Where's that?"

"It's a little town about sixty miles north of here. You gon' live with your half-brother and his family."

"The ones who came to see us a while back?"

"Yes.

I guess Winfred and Lilly had decided to keep me. We packed up what little bit I had and walked into the town of Bruce. All I really had were the clothes on my back and a sackful of more old, ragged clothes.

There were no buses between these small country towns. The only transportation between them at that time was the milk truck. This one ran down Highway 9, stopping along the way to pick up milk and eggs from the farms who sold it to the powdered milk factory there in Pontotoc. The milk would be in ten-gallon milk cans, the same kind sold today as antiques. This truck also carried the U.S. mail. They'd even pick up chickens if people had those to transport. Anybody who wanted a ride and had cash could also jump aboard.

The truck appeared to have been an old chicken-coop school bus at one time. It wasn't an open truck; there was a top on it, in case it rained. A row of windows down the side allowed for a breeze.

Dub and Dad walked with me down to where the milk truck picked me up. Even though I loved them, the excitement of going to a new home suppressed any sadness I felt about leaving the log cabin behind. As Dad put me on the truck, he said, "Son, stay out of trouble. You're not worth a plug nickel, but I wouldn't take a million dollars for you." He gave the driver instructions on where to drop me off. The driver knew everybody along the road between Bruce and Pontotoc, so he knew exactly where to take me. When the truck pulled off, I yelled out "Good-bye!" to Dub, and we kept waving and waving at each other.

That truck must've made a thousand stops, picking up eggs, milk, chickens and mail. Having always had to walk everywhere I went, riding was a real pleasure for me. The chickens and other things on board didn't bother me at all. I was used to that. After all, I had just finished the fourth grade, and had grown up in the country.

It was just before dark. We'd ridden about twelve miles outside of Bruce when the driver turned to me and said, "This here's your stop."

"Is this Pontotoc?"

"Naw, this is where your Aunt Nan lives." I remembered Dad mentioning something about her, but I'd forgotten I was supposed to stop and visit with her.

Beside the road was a smiling woman who looked very much like my father. "You must be Joe Abb," she said. "I'm your Aunt Nan, your dad's sister."

"Yes'm. Hello, ma'am."

Aunt Nan lived in a big, old country house surrounded by a large

90

orchard of fruit trees. Peaches, pears, plums—you could hardly see the house, sitting back off the road, for all the trees. Behind the house was a big barn. I was all eyes. This seemed to be a very large farm. Aunt Nan was a widow, and lived with her daughter and son-in-law in this big house. The house belonged to them. We all had a big supper, then it was time to get ready for bed.

The next day was Sunday, and we went to an all-day singing at the nearby wooden country church with dinner on the grounds afterward. This was a once-a-year event. Everybody had on their best clothes. All the ladies were in dresses, some of the men had on suits and ties, while others wore the usual bib overalls. I ate my fill of all that good food before heading back to spend another night with Aunt Nan and her family.

Early Monday morning, the milk truck came by again, and Aunt Nan put me back on it for the rest of the trip to Pontotoc. Those chickens cackling did not bother me, but there were two women on board this leg of the journey, sitting between the two chicken coops. Nice-looking young ladies wearing bright red lipstick. They were not satisfied with the ride. I listened to them talking. Both had just gotten married, and their husbands were in the Army about sixty miles away. We rode along on that gravel road, stopping and starting every five or ten miles to pick up more cargo.

Finally, about mid-morning, we got to a crossroads with two stores. "Joe Abb Overby?" said the driver. "This here's your stop."

"Is this Pontotoc?"

"Naw, just outside of it. But this is where you're supposed to get off."

I jumped down on the ground and looked around. There was a cute little girl, about 14 years old, standing there who kept looking at me. She had long, dark hair, worn Lana Turner style, and was wearing a one-piece suit with a big collar, like a Quaker. I said, "I'm lookin' for Winfred Overby."

"You must be Joe Abb Overby."

"That's right. That's me." I was never at a loss for words.

"I'm supposed to take you home with me. We live about half a mile down this gravel road. My daddy's Winfred Overby."

"Who are you?"

"I'm Ruby." If Winfred was this girl's father, I was actually her uncle, even though I was younger than her. This was the first time I'd heard about Winfred having any children. It was a surprise to me. I was thinking, "What am I going to do? I'll be living in a house with a *girl*!" It was unbelievable.

All these years, I'd lived in the log cabin with Dad, Dub, and John. Dad hadn't allowed us to use bad language, but if I wanted to pass gas or go outside and take a leak, I would let it go. Now, here was a girl who

91

was going to be in the same house. "How am I going to live with this?" I thought.

It was about a twenty-minute walk back to the house. I decided it would be good to impress Ruby.

"I had me a business down in Pittsboro," I told her.

"A business? But you're just a kid! What kind of business would you have?"

"Me and a fellow named Sam Parker, we started a business cuttin' stove wood."

"Stove wood?"

"Yep. We had cords and cords of it stacked up. People had the money, ready to pay us for it, and I may have to go back down there to collect all that money."

"Uh-huh." She didn't seem impressed enough, so I continued on.

"And I had a couple of nice-looking girlfriends down in Bruce, too."

"Girlfriends? At your age?"

"Oh, yeah. One of 'em was named Dorothy Hanniford, and her daddy was our mailman. Another was named Joanne, and another one even cut her curls off and give 'em to me when she heard I was leaving. I forgot to bring 'em with me, but they were real pretty. All them girls liked me, and I liked them."

She listened to my whole tale, then said, "Joe Abb Overby! You are the biggest liar!" I was a pretty good liar, but it was starting to look like I wasn't going to be getting away with very much around Ruby. She continued, "And when we get to the house, you better stay out of my room, you hear?"

"Okay." I'd just come from living in a two-room log cabin, so this concept escaped me.

"What's in my room is mine, and you better stay out of there," she said. "Boys ain't got no business in a girl's room."

"Well, if I gotta stay out of your room, then you're gon' stay out of mine."

"Oh, no, I'm not."

"Why not? What's good for the goose is good for the gander."

"You'll see," she said, ending that conversation.

Winfred and Lilly lived on the outskirts of Pontotoc. It was much less rural than where I was used to living; you could walk to the county store up at the crossroads. Pontotoc was also an older town than Bruce, so it had doctors, dentists and other amenities.

When we were approaching the house, I thought it was brick. As we got closer, I could see that it was only some kind of tin siding that had been painted to look like bricks. Nobody else was there, so Ruby showed me around. "This here's the living room," she said as we went in the front door off the porch. It was a big room with a huge fireplace. "We make quilts in the wintertime in here, too," she continued, pointing out where the quilts would be hung from the ceiling during the quilting sessions.

Next came the two bedrooms on the front of the house. "Here's Momma and Daddy's room, and there's mine. You remember to stay out of my room, now, you hear?"

"All right; I said I would. Where am I gonna sleep?"

"We'll get there. This here's the kitchen," she said, leading me through to the middle part of the house. "And here's the cannin' room, where you're gon' sleep." It was a small room off the kitchen on the back of the house.

"I'm gon' sleep there by myself?"

"Well, of course, silly!"

My own room! I was happy as a pig in corn. I'd never lived in a house with five rooms before! A house that size, with a back porch and a front porch, was very impressive. My room was where they kept all the colorful jars of fruits and vegetables that Lilly would can in the summer so we could have them through the winter months. I didn't even care if Ruby went in there, I was so happy.

"There's the back porch, outside." It was just outside the canning room. "And down there's where we draw our water." There was a large well at the end of the porch, where they drew water with a rope and bucket. They had no electricity or running water, but I wasn't used to having these things, anyway, so I didn't miss them. Electricity and city water stopped one house from where we lived. Looked like I was going to still be country, even there in Pontotoc. Ruby went into her room and left me alone to unpack the few rags I'd brought along with me.

I went out on the back porch and explored the rest of the property. Directly behind the house was a garden, and beyond that was the barn. A large woodpile stood next to the barn. There was a pen with a large pig in it next to the garden. Another garden was located to the left of the house. The front yard was bare, as most were in those days. Nobody had the manicured grass lawns like they do today. West of our house were cow pastures, small farms and woods.

Lilly arrived home shortly after Ruby and I got back. It was good to see a somewhat familiar face, and she looked just the same as she had that day they'd come by the log cabin to visit. I helped Lilly milk the cows that evening. "You ever milked a cow before, Joe Abb?" she asked me.

"Naw'm," I said.

"Well, here's how you do it. I'm gon' let you milk these smaller cows, since your hands are smaller." She explained the whole process to me, and I milked my first cow.

When Lilly came back, she also brought with her their baby girl, only eight months old. Her name was Janie Lou. This was another surprise to me. Winfred and Lilly didn't have any boys, only girls. I just fell in love with baby Janie. She was like a baby sister to me. But Ruby was always bossy. She had an attitude similar to the Franklin boys, that I was intruding on her space. I was the type to take over wherever I went, and she didn't like that.

The first few days, Ruby was a little hateful toward me. She did the cooking for the family. When we sat down to dinner that night, Ruby filled plates for Winfred and Lilly and served them at the table. I kept waiting for mine, but she filled her own plate and sat down. "What about me?" I asked.

"You can get your own," said Ruby. Neither Winfred nor Lilly said anything to her about this attitude. I climbed down off my chair and filled my plate. It was a full meal, three or four types of vegetables, including cabbage and black-eyed peas, hot cornbread with butter, and plenty of milk to drink. I guess today it would be called "soul food". Everything came out of the garden or canning room. I was amazed by this. At the cabin, Dub would put everything into one pot and boil it. We only had about two pots to cook in, so everything got cooked together. These vegetables were cooked separately, and seasoned like they should be. Everything had a lot of taste to it.

So, this was to be my next home. I'd lived in the log cabin longer than anywhere, so long that it really had seemed like home. I wondered how long this new home would last.

Chapter 22
Farm Life

Life with Winfred's family may have started out a little rocky, but that seemed to be normal for me. Things soon smoothed out and I adjusted well to farm life.

Lilly was a little bossy, but she had a way of loving you into doing things. She and I had hit it off back at the log cabin, and she set out to teach me how to help her with the farm chores. It was Lilly who taught me how to milk the cows, feed the horses, chickens and hogs, and all the other hundreds of tasks that have to be done every day on a farm. Before my arrival, she had done all the barn work. I took over all the feeding from Lilly.

Feeding the animals was right up my alley. There was a hog in a pen behind the barn. After I fed him, I'd crawl over the fence and scratch his belly. Sometimes I rode him, but he didn't like that. There were eight cows, some horses, the hog and what seemed like about 300 chickens.

It was not long before I became an expert farmhand. Since my hands were small, Lilly let me milk the young cows who'd just had their first calves. They had smaller teats that were better suited to my little hands. There were two young heifers I milked every morning and night, after I fed the other animals. Milking machines had not come into use by this time, so we milked all the cows by hand. I was proud of myself for learning to do all this work, and didn't want anyone to take my job from me. Lilly thought the world of me because she'd been doing it all herself before I got there.

Ruby got up early in the morning and cooked breakfast while Lilly and I headed for the barn. When we finished the barn work, we would walk back to the house, which was about 1,000 feet away. Ruby would have plenty of bacon, eggs, gravy, hot biscuits and hot coffee. Winfred and Baby Janie would still be sleeping. As far as I could see, Lilly, Ruby and I did all the work around there; Winfred did nothing. There was a Negro lady who came in every Wednesday to clean the house. I thought it was strange that she always came in the back door, when everybody else who came to visit entered through the front. I was fond of this lady. She always called me "honey child."

Summertime was canning time. My bedroom was the canning room. It was also where they kept all the canned food. Lilly would take food from the garden in summer and can it so we would have vegetables in the winter months. We hardly ever bought any food. I was eager to learn everything, since I had never really done any work around the log cabin.

Canning was fascinating to me. Lilly gave me several jobs. I washed a lot of the vegetables, helped shell butterbeans and peas, peel tomatoes, shuck corn and cut it off the cob, peel apples, and all the other work that went into canning the fruits and vegetables. One of my jobs was to snap beans and pull the strings off them. I didn't mind doing it at first, but after snapping beans for two or three hours, I really got tired of that.

Lilly and Ruby would put the beans in a pressure cooker. The steam would come out the top of it and whistle. Once the beans were blanched in the boiling water, they'd pour them into the prepared Mason jars, put a rubber gasket around the top, then tighten the metal lids down to seal them. If a jar wasn't sealed, air could get in there and spoil the food inside. You'd see some jars on the shelf with bubbles around the top where they'd spoiled.

I started school in Pontotoc with the 1942-43 school year. My fifth-grade teacher's name was Mrs. Anderson. She looked like a real schoolteacher. Her blonde hair was worn in tight curls against her head from a permanent wave. She was around 50 years old, and didn't really get too involved with us. If we got through with our work early, she would read to us. Her voice would silence us all, and the stories were fascinating. One of my favorites was a story about northern Russia. There was a ten-foot giant who lived way back in the woods and never slept. The sun didn't shine up there too often, and he'd walk through the countryside in the darkness. It was all fiction, of course, but it was scary and I liked it. You could hear a pin drop when she was reading us these stories. She also led us in singing songs, including those from the Broadway show, *Oklahoma!*, which was popular at the time. I really liked that because some of the songs were about cowboys.

For the first time, I did not have to wear bib overalls to school. Lilly bought me pants and shirts and I would help her iron them. We would put three irons on the wood cookstove, heat them up and then she and I would iron everybody's clothes. All my shirts and pants were starched and ironed. I really thought I was somebody! Lilly even bought me a real toothbrush and some toothpaste.

At Pontotoc, grade-school football was big stuff. This was my first experience playing football. Every week, the fifth grade played the sixth grade at lunch hour, in the field in front of the school. We had no equipment, just a football. The field didn't have any markings or goalposts on it, and the games were not really sanctioned by the school. We played tough and hit hard. I played left guard and left tackle. Almost every game, I would get the wind knocked out of me and go to the sidelines. Within five or ten minutes, I would be back in the game. They could not keep me out of that game. Most young boys around there loved to play football.

High school boys would referee and control our games. There were no uniforms or whistles, they just hollered. We would plan each play in the huddle, and we'd either pass or run. The teachers were never around when we played.

The only problem with our football games was that the sixth graders had a boy who had failed two years. His last name was Sledge. He was thirteen years old, while the rest of us were ten or eleven. Nobody could block Sledge. He was so big, and his voice had even started changing. The other sixth graders liked him because he helped them win.

One day we got into our huddle and our quarterback said, "Joe Abb, we gon' move you to right guard. I believe you can stop Sledge. Give 'im all you got, and let 'im know who to hell the boss is in this school."

I said, "Man, I can do that!"

"I'll keep the ball and run through the hole you make."

"All right. Let's do it!"

The ball was snapped. I hit Sledge with everything I had. About five minutes later, I woke up again. "Where am I?"

A high school senior was there watching over me. He said, "You're on the bench. You okay?"

The pain was so bad, I was thinking, "I'll never play football again," but I said, "Yeah." About ten minutes later I was back on the field.

Sledge was every bit his name. That was the last game he played. They relieved him from playing ball with the fifth and sixth graders because he would almost kill us. He and I never talked about this incident, but we'd speak to each other from time to time.

After school, we would ride the school bus home and my work was just beginning. The first chore was to gather about 150 eggs from the henhouse and put them in a big crate on the back porch. When the egg crate was full, about 24 dozen, I would hitch up the horses to the wagon, drive to Pontotoc, drop off the eggs and buy feed for the cows and chickens. This trip was made about once a week. We'd grow our own hay for the cows and horses. The milk cows were also fed cottonseed meal as long as they were giving milk. If they were "dry" cows—not giving milk—they only got hay.

I'd drop off the eggs, pack up the feed, then head the two miles back home. There was one spot along the trip that scared me to death. That was the railroad crossing. The tracks crossed the road at an angle, and the horses and mules really didn't like those trains. I wasn't crazy about them, either. It seemed every time I got close to the railroad track, a train would start coming one way or the other, and they had to blow that loud whistle every time. Whenever they did, those horses would run away. I usually wet all over my pants before I could get them stopped. If I heard a train approaching, I'd try to stop the horses or turn them around.

On one occasion, I just jumped off the wagon and they ran until they ran off the road into the ditch. I finally caught up with them, got back on the wagon and headed home. Thank God I had already delivered all the eggs, or we would've been in a mess.

One day, when I arrived home from delivering the eggs, I noticed that there was a hog that had been butchered and was hanging by his back feet in the back yard. Lilly and Winfred were salting down the carcass. There was no refrigerator, so they had to use salt to preserve the meat.

When I went to feed the animals, I noticed that my pig was gone from his pen, and suddenly realized what had happened. I'd been eating all that good bacon and ham, but it had never occurred to me before where it had come from. It was upsetting; here was an animal I'd actually gotten to know. I even cried a little. Winfred and Lilly never got another pig after that. It wasn't because of me, they just didn't.

One chilly, windy morning, we got up early and one of the cows didn't show up to get her feed. "Joe Abb, go out and look for that cow," said Lilly.

"Where should I look?"

"You know that pine thicket out there between the fields?"

"Yez'm."

"Sometimes, when it's windy, they go out there to calve. Go look there for her. Be careful, too. She may run at you, since she'll have her new calf with her."

This was very exciting for me. I'd never seen a newborn baby calf. I made my way to the pine thicket, and I could feel the cow before I saw her. You'd be amazed at the heat a cow puts off in winter. When I came into the small clearing, she charged me.

"Whoa, girl, it's okay. It's just me. You know me. I'm not gon' hurt you."

When she recognized my voice, she backed off. "What you got here, girl? Did you have your baby?"

I looked and there was the little calf, barely able to stand. He was trying with all his might to find his mother's milk and get his first food.

For me to stand there and watch this, that I'd never seen before, was just great. I was a part of this new family's first hours together.

The little calf staggered over to me. I was so close to the mother, from all those months of feeding her, that she let me touch the calf. He was velvety soft, and let out a little cry.

Eventually, we headed back to the barn. I put them in a warm stall, put plenty of straw around them so they could stay warm, and even brought a pail of water for the mother. It was not long before that baby was eating out of my hand—and also my pockets.

It became my job to look for the baby calves on cold mornings. One morning, I went out to find that one of our horses had a small foal. That really excited me. Within three hours, the little horse was jumping and kicking straight up. He must've hit the ground kicking and running.

Even though I was too young to understand sex, I was beginning to see where the young cows and horses were coming from. I was so excited with the baby animals, where they came from didn't bother me for years to come. The first time I was actually there when one was born, it was amazing to me. I finally got used to it, but the wonder of the moment never left me.

Still in the fifth grade, I was too young to get involved with the little girls. Something inside me clicked, however, and I found myself for the first time looking at the girls. They appeared to be prettier than the boys. One girl kept looking at me and smiling. She would always talk to me. Her name was Martha Harrington The girls always came on to the boys then, and I guess if they hadn't, we'd still have been banging our heads out on the football field. At that age, we would try to sit together on the school bus going home, but we always made it look like it was an accident.

At the end of the school year, Martha came up to me and handed me an envelope. "Here, Joe Abb," she said.

"What's this?"

"It's an invitation to my birthday party. I hope you can come." She smiled so pretty at me that I knew I would go. Martha was a tiny girl for her age, and very pretty.

I took the invitation home and gave it to Ruby. "What's this for?" I asked her.

She opened the envelope and looked at the invitation. "Why, it's an invitation to Martha Harrington's birthday party! What fun!"

"What do they do at a birthday party?"

"Joe Abb, you never been to a birthday party before?"

"No."

"Well, then you just *have* to go! They play games, and eat cake and ice cream."

"That sounds like fun."

"Oh, it is!" She called down the hallway of the house, "Momma! Joe Abb's been invited to Martha Harrington's birthday party."

"Well, how 'bout that?" said Lilly. She took the invitation and looked at it. "I think it'd be alright for him to go to this."

When the day of the party came, Lilly and Ruby got me all cleaned up and dressed for the party. "Now, Joe, don't you use any bad language at the party. There's gon' be girls there."

"I know that."

"And don't say anything bad about people."

"I won't!" This party seemed to be more trouble than it was worth—or, at least, getting ready for it was.

I finally got there, and Martha's sixteen-year-old sister seemed to be taking special notice of where I was, and making sure that I was always near Martha. Their house was nicer than ours. They were upper class in the community, and they lived close enough to Pontotoc that they had running water and electricity. They even had a windmill in the back yard. It was interesting to me, but I wasn't envious of them for it. I'd had those things in the orphans' home in Jackson, and I'd lived without them, too.

When we played games, Martha's sister rigged everything so we were partners. The games all seemed to involve things like holding hands and walking around the house. When it was time to eat, Martha's sister again made sure I was sitting next to her. There were cookies and lots of ice cream, made with a hand-cranked freezer.

After the party, I'd see Martha on Sundays, when she and some of her girlfriends would walk down the road past our house. We still sat together on the school bus the following year in school, too.

With school ending, I needed to find myself some boys to play with over the summer. Winfred owned a 40-acre piece of land that we farmed, and alongside that another 80 acres. On the back side of the 80 acres lived a family, the Kaisers, who rented an old wooden house with no water or electricity. The mother, who everybody called "Maw", was in her late thirties. She had one son in the Army, Clarence, and her son Earl was in the CCC camp. "CCC" stood for Civilian Conservation Corps, and was another of President Roosevelt's programs started to give young boys a job. They got paid about $22 a month, but had to send half of it back home to their parents. Maw was a widow, whose husband had been gassed in World War I and died young. She got an additional $4 a month from her husband having been a veteran.

At home, Maw had three boys. Parker was 12 years old and good looking, but he didn't dress very well. The family was too poor. He used to read comic books all the time, especially Dick Tracy. Even though he was

100

a good reader and writer, he didn't have any common sense. But he was so good looking, with dark hair and eyes, that all the girls liked him. Ross was the next boy. He was nine years old, and we used to call him "Mug". Ross was short, and was kind of a dumb follower, with blondish-brown hair. The youngest son was O.T., who we called "Otto", and he was four. Otto had a different father from the others. He was a nice little boy.

There were also two girls in the Kaiser family. Ethel, who we called "Et", was 11. She was skinny and not bad looking, but very plain. None of them ever had anything to dress up in. Et's hair was light brown and hung down around her shoulders in curls. Frances, or "Check", was about 7. She was a pretty blonde girl who I heard many years later had moved down to Biloxi.

I took up with the Kaiser family for the summer. All the kids smoked cigarettes, but I never took up the habit. We would swim in the cow ponds. Parker taught me how to fish and set out trout lines. These were long lines running all the way across the pond. About every five feet, we would place a fish hook. We'd come back the next day and find some catfish on some of the hooks. We'd rebait the hooks and return the next day. That was called "trout line fishing." Usually, about the only thing you'd catch was an old mud catfish. That's about all that lived in those cow ponds. If you ate one of those things, you'd taste mud for a week. Of course, we were kids, and it was more fun than anything.

The 80-acre piece of property that Winfred owned had a cotton farm and plenty of yellow apple trees. But mostly, we worked the chickens, eggs and milk. World War II was in full swing, and you could sell about everything we had on the farm—chickens, eggs, cotton, milk—so we had some money coming in every week. Lilly and I did all the work. I thought it was very important to be in charge and do all the work. When Lilly would brag on me, I would work much harder. It was work I really enjoyed because I had never been able to work on a farm with cattle and other livestock. This situation just seemed perfect to me.

Chapter 23
The Big Show

E ven though we didn't have electricity at the farm, we still listened
to the radio. Winfred and Lilly had a battery-operated radio, just
like the one the Easleys used to have. Lilly always listen to Gene Steele's
show from Memphis. We sometimes listened to the Grand Ole Opry on
Saturday nights. Everybody in that part of the country did back then. It
was a country music show, and that was about the only kind of music you
heard in Mississippi.

Ruby, however, liked a show that came on another station at the same
time, called *Your Hit Parade*. She liked to hear singers like Frank Sinatra
that appeared on that show. I didn't care too much for him, but I did like
to hear Bing Crosby sing. Our news came from the radio, too, courtesy of
Walter Winchell and, of course, Winfred's favorite, H.B. Calvin.

Instead of getting the *Grit* newspaper, Winfred and Lilly subscribed to
Collier's magazine. We'd get a new issue every week. Hitler seemed to be
in the news all the time, as well as Winston Churchill. After Pearl Harbor,
there was also more about the Japanese Emperor, Hirohito, and his white
horse. General Nimitz said when we conquered Japan he was going to ride
that white horse down the streets of Tokyo.

I started seeing big billboards posted on the barns along the old country
roads about a show coming near Pontotoc in about a month. "COME SEE
THE GRAND OLE OPRY STARS," they said. There were more flyers
about the show tacked up on telephone poles. Everybody was talking about
it. I asked if I could have the money to go see my idols like Roy Acuff,
the Smokey Mountain Boys, Ernest Tubb, the Texas Troubadours and the
Carter Family.

"If you work extra, you can earn the money," said Winfred. "How
much does it cost?"

"The bus ride there is fifty cents, and it's another fifty cents to get in."

"Well, we got all them apples out there. Why don't you pick some of
them and sell 'em in town?"

"Okay, I can do that." I set out to pick apples and sell them on the
weekends. They weren't hard to sell, but I had to carry a large sack of

them on my back around town all weekend. Pretty soon, I'd sold all my golden apples, and was looking forward to seeing the Grand Ole Opry stars perform live in concert.

The day finally came. I walked about a mile before sunup to catch a bus, another of those old chicken-coop school buses somebody had. We paid fifty cents to get on the bus and headed halfway across the country to get to where the show was going to be. It was a fenced-in cow pasture, but you had to pay to get in before you got off the bus.

Along the way, the bus stopped at every gravel road crossing, picking up all kinds of country folks. By the time we got there, it was about 10:30 in the morning. It was a big thing. You could smell whiskey on everybody's breath over about the age of 16. We could all tell it was going to be a hell-raising party. I paid my fifty cents as I got off the bus and started walking across the cow pasture toward the stage. As I did, I could already hear the music playing. They had already started the show.

All the buses, about ten or fifteen of them, had parked along the roadside by the cow pasture. Some people had driven their own cars or trucks. There were probably about 500 people there. Most of the men were in bib overalls, but I had worn regular pants and a shirt.

The stage was built about eight feet high, on some old telephone poles. You could see and hear everything really well. By the time I got to the stage, I had stepped in about five piles of cow shit. I was in such a hurry, I didn't want to miss even one song.

Some no-name guy was playing on stage when I got there. He was just a warm-up act, but he was wearing the prettiest Texas boots I'd ever seen. They were like something you'd see in the movies, black with stars on them. He had on a blue cowboy suit with red stars and sparkles on it, and a cowboy hat that also sparkled. The singer was maybe 21 years old, certainly no more. His guitar looked like it was made of diamonds, and he could actually sing pretty well.

Most of the people at the concert were older than me. There were quite a few young country girls in the crowd kissing and hanging onto their boyfriends. The war had really brought people out of the country and put them into these types of places where there was music, whiskey and everything. Most of the boys were waiting to be called into the Army, Navy or Marines. If they had turned 18 years old, it was a matter of days before the Army would get them, so the boys and girls were drinking moonshine and having a big party. I pretty much kept to myself.

Since this was right out in the middle of a cow pasture, everybody's shoes were covered with cow shit. But the more moonshine they drank, they didn't really give a damn. Drinking all that moonshine also sent people to the outhouses. There was one to the left for the men, and another to the right for the ladies. The men's outhouse was a two-holer, but most of the men were just urinating on the ground beside it. Even so, there was still a line a mile long to get into it.

After relieving myself, I headed back to the stage, so as not to miss any of that good music. I'd picked and sold a lot of apples to get there, and wanted my hard-earned fifty cents' worth. A different band was on stage. No singers, just square dance and fiddle music. This progression of acts continued into the late afternoon, but still no big stars had shown up. I had come to see Roy Acuff and Ernest Tubbs.

Finally, I climbed up on the corner of the stage and yelled out to the announcer, "Where is Roy Acuff and Ernest Tubbs?"

The whole crowd could hear me, and they started to get unruly. They all wanted to know the same thing. The announcer glared at me, and right away the band started playing some good hoedown music and turned up the sound really loud. The square dancers came out, in bright red dresses with petticoats, and were kicking up their heels.

Before I knew what was happening, a guy grabbed me by the neck because I'd almost started a fight by asking where the big stars were. He said, "You little sonofabitch, get off the stage or I'll kick yer ass all the way back to that little town called Pontotoc!" The guy spoke with a Yankee accent. I quickly left the stage.

After the square dancers and loud music stopped, the announcer came to the microphone again. "We're sorry, folks, but there's been a bus accident, and the stars are gon' be a little late gettin' here." The crowd let out an audible moan and started grumbling. "So please just hang in there with us," the announcer continued. He didn't want a riot on his hands.

About an hour later, the Carter Family showed up and did a wonderful show. Everybody enjoyed them very much. Mother Maybelle was playing a strange-looking instrument I'd never seen before. It had a beautiful sound. I later found out that it was called an autoharp. As soon as the Carter Family finished playing, the concert was over. No other big stars ever showed. The crowd wasn't happy, but the promoters were the ones to blame, and they were nowhere in sight.

We all headed back to the buses. It took us about half an hour to get everyone on because the driver got mad and told everyone, "Clear that dang cow shit off your feet before you get on my bus!"

When the bus arrived in Pontotoc, I still had to walk the two miles back to the farm. I actually got home in time to milk the cows and gather all those eggs. It had been a long day for me, and I slept well that night. But I was still mad that I hadn't gotten to see Roy Acuff and the Smokey Mountain Boys.

🌲
Chapter 24
Brothers in Transition

Not long after the Grand Ole Opry concert, brother Dub showed up to live with us on the farm. I'd been there all alone until he came to help. Even though he did quite a bit of work around the place, I was the one in charge of all the farm animals. Nobody was going to take that job away from me.

Dub got along pretty well with Ruby. They were closer in age than she and I were. He would do whatever she asked of him. Even so, Dub kept to himself most of the time he was with us. He and I got along well, and seldom got into fights. We kind of enjoyed seeing each other again; he was my bigger brother. Dub always wanted to make sure I was okay. But I don't think he ever liked living with us there as much as he liked being in the log cabin with our dad.

I had not heard anything from our dad until Dub showed up. He said Dad was getting much older and nobody had answered any of those other letters he'd sent to our other half brothers to take any of us boys. John had gone back to Jackson to live with the rich lady, and Dad was now by himself. That was really the way he wanted it to be.

Dub and I were together again! We slept in my room, the canning room, in my bed. I was glad he came to live with us. He was still trying to teach me right from wrong. Whenever I'd do something bad, I'd hear that familiar admonishment, "The devil's gon' get you, Joe Abb!"

Fall was coming on and the weather was getting a little cooler. We had to start building fires in the fireplace. Dub's job was to get all the wood for the cookstove and all the fireplace wood to heat the house. Of course, I helped. School started and Dub went there with us. He was in the seventh or eighth grade.

Each day when we got home from school, we had to hitch up the sled to haul the wood. It was an old homemade sled we'd hook onto our horse named Nell. Nell was a big, black mare, a workhorse. Before I had come to the farm, Nell had been Ruby's horse, but she had become mine. After all, I had been taking care of her for over a year. Winfred had started me out riding her by putting me up on her back and leading her around. I always rode bareback. The other horse, Daisy, was smaller, and couldn't

105

be used for the kind of work we were doing.

Nell was as gentle as she could be. On Sundays, I'd ride her off the farm, down a dirt road into the woods. We'd go up to a wooden bridge there, then turn around. She seemed to be uncertain about crossing that bridge, so I didn't make her go over it.

I also did all the cattle driving with old Nell. When the ponds would dry up in summer, we had to drive the cattle from where they grazed to where they could drink. Sometimes a cow or bull would run away and Nell and I would have to get tough and bring them back into line. It seemed like Nell knew exactly what to do. When to run, when to stop, and when to almost run over some of those big, tough bulls was second nature to her. The bulls would sometimes get a little mean, and we'd have to do some tough riding to get them back into the herd.

One time, the chase was on with a bull we were trying to keep from getting into a green pasture where he wasn't supposed to be. I headed Nell straight for him, and we hit hard. The bull went down, while Nell and I were still standing. She was twice as big as that bull. He got the message, and went back with the herd. Once the cattle got their bellies full of water, we headed back to the south forty.

On the way back, everything was going really well. No cattle were getting out of line. All of a sudden, Nell reared up on her hind legs and let out a big whinny. Off I slid, hitting the ground so hard it knocked the wind right out of me. When I got my breath back, I looked over and Nell was standing about fifty feet from me. She was such a good horse, I could not understand why she had thrown me. It finally occurred to me that she had probably almost stepped on a snake. Horses can detect snakes, and are deathly afraid of them. I never did see the snake myself; the grass was too high. It must have slithered away.

Now, I had a problem. Nell was so big, I could not get back onto her back to ride her home to the barn. The cattle were all grazing in the same spot, so there was no danger of their running away. I finally led Nell up to a tree stump, climbed back on and headed the cattle back to the barn. I'd only been rounding up cattle a few months through the summer, and was far from an expert, but we made it back to the pasture safely.

Dub was waiting for me and Nell to take the sled into the woods to cut wood. We had a cross-cut saw, with Dub on one end and me on the other. He would pull and I would push. That was hard, hard work, but we were good at it. We certainly had plenty of practice.

Once we had cut enough wood, we'd load it up on the sled, and Nell would carry us back to the house. Dub and I would get on the sled with the wood, and back we'd go. There was a large woodpile between the chicken house and the farmhouse. We'd offload the wood there, then I would take Nell back to the barn, take all the harnesses off her and put them in her stall with her. When I put her in the stall, I'd always give her extra hay because she was my horse and I loved her very much.

After putting Nell in the barn, I'd return to the woodpile, where we'd split the wood we'd just cut. We used a sledgehammer, wedge and axe to do this. Brother Dub was not the heavy worker I was. Even though he was older than me, he just couldn't split the wood like I could. We were about the same size, but Dub just wasn't tough. He didn't play football with us at school, either.

The rain started to fall, and eventually all the cow ponds filled up with water. That meant no more herding of cattle down to the big cow pond on the south eighty. I didn't especially like herding because I had to get down off old Nell, open the gaps to the south eighty, run the cows through the gap, then find a way to get back on old Nell. While I was climbing back on the horse, the cattle would stray, especially those bad bulls. But once the rain came down and filled all the cow ponds, cattle herding was over for the rest of the year.

That was an election year for state senators, and there was a political rally in Pontotoc one Saturday, with Senator Theodore Gilmore Bilbo himself coming. I'd never been all that interested in politics, but I went because it was a big deal in town, and they were going to have country music before the speeches.

A huge crowd had gathered in front of the courthouse for the rally. There was a stage set up on the courthouse steps, covered with red-white-and-blue bunting. Flags were waving everywhere. I moved away from Winfred and Lilly, lost in the festivities, and stood by myself in the crowd. The country band played for about an hour. Next, a local man got up to introduce the senator and tell us all how great he was, and all the things he'd done for the state. People were cheering, screaming and hollering all around me.

Senator Bilbo finally stepped up to the microphone. He was a small, thin-lipped wiry-looking man wearing a straw hat, white suit pants, a tie, white shirt without a jacket or vest, a red garter on his upper arm and big, wire-framed spectacles on his face. His shirt sleeves were rolled up due to the summer heat. Senator Bilbo's speech seemed to center around keeping colored people and white people apart from each other. He was practically shouting, and gesturing wildly with his hands.

"You see that colored boy over there?" he said, pointing to a young Negro boy sitting by himself over on the town hall steps. "That's where I'm gon' keep 'em! I'm gon' keep things segregated here in this great state of Mississippi!" The crowd cheered and clapped. I looked over at the little Negro boy, just a little younger than me, sitting on the steps. He looked back at me, and we both just grinned and started clapping with everybody

107

else.

Of course, I'd heard other people talking about the "niggas" and what a problem they were, but I'd never had any problems with them. I kept thinking of that hard-working old Negro farmer driving his team of oxen with such expertise, and the kind colored lady who'd given Lolly and me food when we were so hungry. Why, my own family had given me more trouble than either of them.

The senator's speech continued. "Vote for me, send me back to Washington, and I'll keep them niggas in their place!" The crowd cheered again. "And I'll tell you one more thing, I can eat more watermelon than my opponent any day!" This was met with laughs and wild cheers, since watermelon was a big crop in that area. The senator's speech didn't interest me; all I'd been interested in was hearing that good country music.

When the rally was over, everybody was all excited that we'd been visited by Senator Bilbo himself. That was all the townspeople could talk about for weeks. I didn't get why everybody was so crazy about him. To me, he'd seemed like a great actor who could get the crowd all riled up. It seemed like he ought to be in show business. What he had to say really didn't have any effect on my day-to-day life; I had my own problems then.

As the months ticked along and winter closed in on us, Dub was sent back to live with our dad in the log cabin. I never understood why this was. One day, he was packing his clothes, putting his arms around me and saying goodbye. It seemed we were always saying goodbye. It was Winfred who wanted to get rid of Dub; he didn't do as much work as me, and Winfred wanted somebody he could put to work.

I kept feeding chickens and milking cows, feeding cattle, gathering eggs and playing football with my school friends. But deep in my heart, I was very sad that Dub was gone. At night, I would look over at his side of the bed and wonder if he was all right. I had no place to go except to stay where I was, there at the farmhouse with my half-brother and his family. Every night, I would think, "Where is Dub?" and go to sleep dreaming he was okay.

Christmas time arrived again. We didn't have a tree, but we did get stockings and leave them by the fireplace on Christmas Eve. Next morning, there were presents in them. Lilly said that Santa had left them. I knew better, but didn't want to ruin it for the other kids. They gave me a flashlight and my first football. I was so proud of those gifts! They were the nicest ones I'd ever gotten for Christmas.

Just after Christmas, my brother John popped up out of nowhere. He had been living with the rich lady in Jackson, or maybe with my dad at the log cabin; I wasn't sure.

Things were getting a little strange. I was thinking something was not right, living with my half brother. Winfred had just gotten rid of Dub, and now here came John, who's eighteen months older than I am. John and I were both pretty hard workers, but Dub wasn't as much so. Winfred wanted to put us to work, and he could not control Dub the way he could control us because we were younger. I thought I was doing pretty good, still hanging in there. I had a place to eat, a place to sleep and a place to go to school. It made me think, "Someone must really like me!"

About two weeks after John arrived, Winfred and Lilly sat us all down and said, "We are sellin' this place and movin' to the Mississippi delta."

In reality, Winfred had spent all the money we were making and had run up a lot of debts. He and Lilly had been forced to sell the farm to pay them off, but he would never have told us this. Lilly's father had given them that place, and he would have been very angry to know how Winfred had mismanaged it. Mr. Dorman owned a country store, and had managed a Kroger in Shelby, Mississippi at one time. Winfred secretly sold the place—land, cows, chickens, everything except the farm equipment, our household furnishings, two mules and my Nell, who he'd be needing to plow the land in the delta.

This news of the move did not sit well with me. I loved going to school at Pontotoc and had many friends there. But what could I do, an eleven-year-old boy?

We headed for the Mississippi delta, all the way over on the west side of the state—big cotton country. Winfred used some of the proceeds from the sale of the farm to hire a truck to move us there. It had big sidebeds that were covered on the sides, but no roof on it. The two mules rode in the back of the truck with the farm equipment. I rode over with the first load, with the truck driver and his friend.

We left early in the morning, heading west on Highway 6. The road took us through Oxford, right by the University of Mississippi. The driver said, "That's the big university, where everybody gets educated." The weather was cold and blustery all the way over, and all the hickories and other hardwood trees were bare. Already, I didn't like the delta. It was nothing like the beautiful forests I'd known in the east, filled with green trees and colorful wildlife.

Around four in the afternoon, we arrived at a place called Hill House, which was near our destination. It wasn't really a town of any size. They had a little general store with a post office inside. The lady who ran the store also drove the local school bus. There was a cotton gin next to a train depot, where trains would stop to pick up the cotton. Cotton gins were all over the delta. The place we were going to be living was about two miles outside of Hill House. All the land around was farmland, mainly farmed by Negroes. White people were about one thirtieth of the population in the delta.

The largest town around was called Clarksdale. It was about eight miles north of Hill House. I remember seeing the sign going into town that said, "Welcome to Clarksdale. Population 14,449". That was the biggest town I'd ever seen. There was even a seven-story building in it. I know because I counted every floor of it when we went by. The truck driver was almost like a tour guide for me. "This is where all the cotton buyers come to inspect and buy bales of cotton from the local farmers," he said. The main highway out of Clarksdale going south ran alongside the levee of the Mississippi River, the "Mighty Mississip".

Levees kept the floodwaters from flooding the rich farmland. They were probably half a mile to a mile back from the river itself. All the houses built on the other side of the levee were on poles about twenty feet above the ground. At a certain part of the year, it always flooded there. The old house we moved into was about another mile back from the levee. It was a big, white house, nicer than the sharecroppers' shacks I'd lived in before, more like the farmhouse we'd just moved from. The only furniture we'd brought with us was the beds.

The Kaiser family that lived in Pontotoc with us, on Winfred's place there, moved with us to the delta. Maw Kaiser and her five kids were going to work with Winfred on the cotton farm and get rich. He had told them we were going to make all kinds of money. Of the five kids, all were big enough to work except one. So my half-brother was looking at having plenty of child labor to run that cotton farm and make himself a lot of money. He was going to be the big boss and take care of everybody's money.

Across the road was a little sharecroppers' house where the Kaisers settled. Again, none of us had running water or electricity there. It was winter time, so we were getting awfully cold. We'd moved from Pontotoc when school was out for the Christmas holidays, so in two weeks we all started back to school.

We had to travel down our dirt road, then another mile or two on a gravel road, Highway 1, then catch a bus for over twenty-something miles to a school in Gunnison. About twelve families lived on that dirt road. When the rain started to come down, that dirt turned into Mississippi gumbo mud. I had heard about it, and now here I was, right in the middle of it. Pontotoc had been up in the hills; it was a nice little town with paved streets and everything. But here in the delta, it was so muddy you could hardly walk when it rained. We'd never had mud like this in Pontotoc.

The way we got to school was new for me. I'm probably one of the only people who ever rode a covered wagon to school. It was pulled by two mules, and looked just like those Conestoga wagons in the old westerns. The guy who owned the wagon lived along the levee. The other kids referred to those people as "river rats". We'd ride the covered wagon down

110

the dirt road to the gravel road, where it would drop us off for the school bus to pick us up. The school buses in the delta were like the modern ones, all sheet metal. No more of the chicken-coop buses, like we'd had farther east. We had to get on the wagon before daylight, and it was freezing.

At each stop, the last boy over twelve years old had to take a large stick, shaped something like a baseball bat, and clean the gumbo mud off the wheels of the wagon before he got on board. The wagon would get so bogged down with that mud on the wheels, it could hardly move. Its wheels were just wooden spoked wheels, just like the pioneers had driven. The driver was supposed to clean this mud off the wheels, but he always made the kids do it. At our stop, it was Parker who got the job.

Inside the wagon was a smudge pot they'd light to keep us warm. It burned charcoal, so it didn't smoke. Fortunately, we were the last house on the dirt road before we got to the gravel road, so we didn't have far to ride in the wagon. Nobody ever took a bath in the winter, and there would be quite an odor in that wagon by the time we got to the bus stop. Everybody would be bundled up in heavy coats, hats, scarves, gloves and gum boots.

While we were waiting on the wagon to pick us up, early in the darkness of the morning, we would all wait inside the house. Only one person would wait outside and listen for the chase chains on the wagon to rattle. Then the lookout would shout, "The wagon is comin'! The wagon is comin'!" Chase chains were chains hooked to the wagon, then hooked to the mules to pull the wagon. You could hear them rattling long before you could see the mules and wagon. They made a chinging sound that carried through the cold morning air.

We'd only lived in this house for a month or two when we found out that we had moved into the wrong house. The real house we were supposed to be in was about four or five miles away! Once again, we loaded up our things into a wagon, hitched up the two mules we'd bought there, named Tom and George, and headed down the road.

Chapter 25
Life in the Delta

Brother John and I drove Tom and George to the new house by ourselves. It was near a town called Alligator, Mississippi. John was in the eighth grade at this time, and I was in the sixth.

We left the farmhouse about daybreak. The wagon was loaded as high as it could be with the farm equipment, beds, dressers, a cookstove, washtubs, and Ruby's cedar chest. On the rear of the wagon was a long pole, almost like a telephone pole, but not nearly as big, sticking out five feet at about a sixty-degree angle. The pole was part of the wagon's bed, and its purpose was to hang the cotton scales so you could weigh the cotton. People got paid for picking cotton based on its weight. The landowner would hang the scale on this pole to weigh each picker's cotton sack, then they'd get paid by how much they'd picked.

John had strapped an old saddle onto the pole, and while I was driving the team, he'd ride on that saddle at the rear of the wagon. After a while, he gave me a turn at it, then we took turns for the rest of the journey.

Just past the town of Alligator, the road straightened out. It had been pretty crooked up to that point. A long straight section spread out ahead of us for about a mile, running parallel to a railroad track for the Illinois Central line. Cotton fields were on both sides. This made me a little nervous after my experience in Pontotoc with mules and trains.

It was nice to be alone with my brother, no adults around to boss us, just driving down that gravel road with a wagon and team of mules. I was driving and John was in the saddle when a freight train came along. It seemed to be doing about ninety miles an hour. That train let out a loud whistle that, combined with the loud engine noise, scared the mules. They started to run away, all while I had the reins. Why did it have to be my luck to be driving when the train came by?

As the mules took off, my fear got the better of me, and I jumped off the side of the wagon. My neck and shoulders hit the hard ground in the ditch at the side of the road. Then I rolled over and looked up to see John riding by me on that saddle, high in the air, hanging on for dear life. "Aaaaaaa!" he yelled as the wagon careened down the road. "Dammit, Joe! Whoa, mules! *Whoa!*"

It didn't take long for the freight train to pass and move on out of sight. The mules had stopped and were just standing there, about four hundred feed down the road from where I'd landed in the ditch. I got on my feet and ran toward the wagon and mules.

By the time I arrived, John had everything under control. He'd ridden that saddle until the wagon had come to a stop. "Dammit, Joe!" he said as he kicked me. "That was all your fault! You don't know from nothin' how to drive a damn team of mules!"

He was exactly right. I was always really afraid of those mules. They were big and mean. We'd even heard that they'd killed somebody years before. I couldn't say anything in response as he cussed me out for letting the mules get away.

Amazingly, nothing was lost off the wagon. John had gotten the mules settled down, and took charge of the driving the rest of the way. We both sat up front; I was too afraid to ride in that saddle on the back any more.

After a few minutes, I started giggling. "What're you laughin' about?" he asked.

"Just thinkin' 'bout you, goin' by on that saddle. You looked pretty scared!"

"Scared? Heck, no, I was just tryin' to hang on! If I'da fell off, I'da been killed!" Then he started laughing, too. "What about you, rollin' over there in the ditch? Your clothes're filthy! *You* was the one scared – why, you wouldn't even stay on the wagon!"

"Yeah, I was scared, alright."

John pulled out a can of Prince Albert smoking tobacco and said, "Joe Abb, I'm gonna let you roll yourself a smoke. You sho' need one."

Even though all the Kaiser kids smoked, I was never a big smoker. John smoked all the time. We were almost there, so all the bad things were over. As we put distance between ourselves and that freight train, we started to relax.

Just about the time we lit up our roll-your-own smokes, here came another train from the opposite direction, blowing that danged horn! John was in charge this time, though. He grabbed the whip and smacked both mules across the ass. They took off running as fast as they could, and we passed the train in no time. John kept that whip on their asses until the train had passed. About half a mile farther, the road made a turn and crossed that railroad track, then headed east, far away from it.

We finally arrived at the new house. "New" is a misleading term. This house was really bad. It was another shotgun house with four rooms, two on either side of a hallway down the center. It still had no heat, electricity or running water. There was an old hand pump in the back yard. I went over and pumped some water, then said, "Ooh! The water's bad here. It smells like rotten eggs and iron!"

"Must be a really shallow well," said John. "Some people actually drink that stuff."

"Yuck! Not me!"

John and I unloaded a few of the smaller things from the wagon, but we would need help to get the heavy items. We spent the night alone in the house.

Winfred rode Nell over the next day and helped us unload the rest of the furniture and farm equipment. We were able to find a farmer about an eighth of a mile down the road who had an Artesian well that gave fairly decent drinking water.

My trip to the new house with John was the only one I made to haul our things there because I couldn't handle the mules past those railroad tracks. John and Winfred made three or four trips. They had to bring saws, axes, plows another wagon torn apart, and everything else in that one wagon. There was even a cow they tied to the back of it. They finally got it all over to the house, where we were going to make all this money on the cotton farm. The whole move took them about a week.

We finally seemed settled in this 80-acre farm. It was located about four miles back off the Mississippi River, back from what they called the "seep waters", so it was fairly good farmland back there. The seep waters would seep through the levee and flood the land up to your ankles, but we didn't have any flooding to speak of where we were. Winfred put us all to work immediately, plowing the fields and getting them ready to plant cotton.

One more time, we started attending a new school. It was in a little town called Duncan. We had to go right through the town of Alligator to get there. We worked the fields mostly, and rarely went to school. This bothered me because I liked going to school and playing sports. I was used to going to school, but now all we did was work those old cotton fields. We didn't know it at the time but that was Winfred's plan, to put John and me to work in the cotton fields, making him rich. The only time he ever sent us to school was when the authorities made him. Just as often, though, they didn't.

The Kaiser family was also a part of Winfred's master plan. He had agreed to give her the income from ten acres of cotton land at the end of the year. But we all had to work all the land together. It wasn't too bad of a deal for her.

When the rains came and the ground was too wet to work, Parker and Mug Kaiser, John and I would play together. But the rest of the time, Winfred was working us hard.

There is a certain time of the year when you plow cotton, another when you hoe it, another when you chop it, and another when you pick it. But while the cotton is growing, you have a time called "lay-by" time. After you get all the weeds out of the fields and get through plowing, there are about three to four weeks when the cotton stalks just grow. That gave us kids time to go to the swimming hole, catch fish and things like that.

The swimming hole here in the delta was different from the cow ponds we'd been swimming in before. This one was called the slough, or the bayou. It was about half a mile away from the house. There were some cypress logs there, and they were very large, about two feet across and eight feet long. We used them to play "battleships".

In this game, we would straddle these large, floating logs and hold a long cane pole in our hands, put it down in the mud at the bottom of the bayou to get momentum on the logs, then head directly for each other. Those logs were big and heavy. When they'd hit, there'd be a big "bang!" and somebody would fall off their log into the water. Sometimes, both guys fell off. We'd play battleships for hours.

The water was only three or four feet deep, so in no time you were back on your log and doing it all over again. We had heard that there were alligators out there in those swamps, but we never saw any. There were lots of water moccasins, though. We'd just pick them up and throw them out of the creek.

When the weather was dry and the bayou got muddy, the fish would stick their heads up out of the mud, and you could catch them. Sometimes, when you'd grab at a fish, it would be a snake instead. Amazingly, none of us ever got bitten.

Of course, we were always buck-ass naked in the bayou. We always swam naked. Nobody had bathing suits.

One Sunday, we were playing battleships and I had gotten what I thought was the biggest log in the bayou. I was so sure that nobody would knock me off that I didn't take off my clothes.

"Hey, Joe Abb, ain't you gon' take off your clothes?" said Parker.

"Naw, Park. Ain't nobody gon' knock me off today!"

"We'll see about *that!*"

I'd issued a challenge too good to resist. The battle started. Bam! I was rammed hard on one side, then bam! on the other. Off I came into the water, clothes and all.

Everybody was laughing at me. "Ha! Ain't nobody gon' knock you off, huh? What you gon' do now?"

I waded ashore, took my clothes off and gathered some bamboo cane. Bamboo grew all through the bayou. Everybody smoked, so there were plenty of matches. I built a fire and hung my clothes over it to dry. They'd smell smoky, but at least they'd be dry.

While my clothes were drying, I got back on my log to do more battle. Now, I was naked like all the rest of the boys.

After about an hour, somebody yelled, "Joe Abb, your clothes're on fire!"

Sure enough, I looked over and that fire had gotten to my clothes. Everybody was just screaming with laughter now.

"What you gon' do now, Joe Abb? You gon' have to walk home nekkid!" yelled Parker.

"Done burned up 'is clothes. That boy gon' be in big trouble!" laughed Mug.

"Winfred's gon' be mad as a wet hen when you come home nekkid!" said John.

"Glad you guys are havin' so much fun!" I said. "Now, who's gon' loan me a shirt so's I can get on home?"

They all grabbed their clothes and took off running, laughing at me all the way.

Now, here I was, buck naked, with about half a mile of cotton fields, corn fields, hay fields and ditch banks between me and the house. To make matters worse, it was Sunday evening, when a lot of the Negro teenagers in the area were usually walking through the fields together with their boyfriends or girlfriends. That was where they did their courting. Nobody had any cars or gasoline during the war, so everybody just got together and walked. Somehow, I had to figure out a way to get home across all those fields without anybody seeing me.

I ran to a corn field and looked up and down the rows. Nobody was coming, so I headed for the next area with high cotton. When the coast was clear again, I ran to a ditch bank with some bushes on it. I knew those cotton fields like the back of my hand, so I thought it would be easy. So far, so good. I kept up this "look and go" thing for several tries.

I made it to a corn field, and traveled the distance of it without anybody seeing me. The corn was high. Across a small dirt road from that corn field was a hay field. It wasn't quite so tall. I poked my head out from between the cornstalks and looked up and down the road. Nobody to the left...nobody to the right. I backed up to get a good running start, then took a quick run to get across.

But I'd waited too late to start running. As soon as I started out of the corn field, I saw a group of about six Negro girls about fourteen to sixteen years old. They were about thirty feet away, walking down the dirt road that I was running across. They all started laughing and pointing.

"Look at dat white boy! Look at dat white boy!"

"He ain' got no clothes on!"

"That boy ain' got no clothes on!"

"Look at dat boy—he ain't got no dick!"

"White boys ain't got no dicks!"

That scared the daylights out of me. I kept running, and they kept yelling.

"Come on back, white boy! What you 'fraid of? Us colored girls?"

I was running as fast as I could, and it seemed like that road was about a mile wide.

Finally, I reached the bushes on the ditch bank at the other side, but I never slowed down until I got home. Those girls kept pointing and hollering, but I never looked back. I went out of sight, and they were still hollering at me. Somebody else may have seen me, but I was moving so fast I'd never have known it.

When I got to the house, I thought it would be all over. I'd just go through the back door to my room and get another pair of overalls. But the back door was locked. Even worse—I could hear girls' voices inside the house! Ruby was visiting with the Lauderdale girls who lived in an old house down the road. What was I to do now?

I ran like hell back to the corn crib. That was a small house where we kept the corn and feed for the horses and mules. There I was, locked in with girls all around. I sat there for an hour, then saw Lilly come out of the house into the back yard.

"Lilly!" I yelled.

"Joe Abb? Is that you?" she said.

"Yes'm. Lilly, I need you to get me a pair of overalls out of my room."

"What? Where's your clothes?"

"They got burned up at the bayou."

"Burned up? How?"

I told her the whole embarrassing story. She started laughing about midway through. When I'd finished, she went in the house, still laughing and shaking her head, and got me a pair of overalls. Boy, was I happy!

Almost every Sunday after that, I'd see the colored girls out walking. They would all wave at me and giggle with each other. Apparently, word got around in the Negro community about what had happened, so for about a month I was known to the teenage colored girls throughout the corn and cotton fields as "the little white boy that didn't have no dick".

117

Chapter 26
Summer on the Bayou

As the crops were all laid by, we had some time on our hands at night. Our same gang would go frog gigging.

Parker's brother had stolen a carbide light, like the miners wear, from the CC camp and brought it home with him. Carbide lights didn't have a battery in them. You put carbide in a steel container, then poured water in there and put the lid on tight. It made a gas that spewed out through a small hole, and you lit it with a match. Behind the little hole was a reflector that made the light shine out. That's what we used for frog gigging.

That old carbide light would help us spot the big bullfrogs sitting on the banks of the bayous. On a good night, you could get fifty to a hundred big, fat bullfrogs. We would go to an old, vacant sharecropper's house on the farm, about 1500 feet down the dirt road, and get everything ready to cook the frogs' legs before we actually caught them.

First, we cleaned out the fireplace and got the skillets. They were those big, heavy, black, cast iron ones. We got some cold biscuits that Maw Kaiser had left over from that day. Next, we got some butter and grease from our house and some firewood, then set up everything in the vacant house. The adults would be sitting around at our house, playing cards or listening to something like the Grand Ole Opry on the radio. They were just as happy to have us out of their hair.

We made frog gigs out of bamboo poles about twenty feet long. On the end, we fastened a gig. It was like a fork, a hard metal piece with six barbed prongs. That carbide light pitched a straight, long beam. Whoever was wearing it turned his head really slowly until the beam lit up the eyes of a big bullfrog. Once we got one in the spotlight, he would only sit still for a short time, then jump. You had to be quick with the gig. The gigger got the pole right over the frog, then came down on him and jabbed really fast.

Those bayous were pretty dangerous at night, wading into that water in total darkness. There were poisonous snakes and some alligators. All four of us went wading or swimming at once. It's really a miracle nothing ever happened to any of us.

By around ten o'clock at night, we had all the frogs we needed, sacks full of them. Of course, by then we were starving. We started a fire in the fireplace of the old sharecropping house and put butter in the frying pan. One of us sliced those cold biscuits and refried them. In the other skillet, we were frying the frogs' legs. Parker made some gravy and John made some sassafras tea. That was made from the roots of little bushes that grew in the area. It tasted something like root beer, only without the foam. We ate frogs' legs until we were all completely filled up.

Once we were full, the activities of the day began to catch up with us. The front room of the house was used to store some of the cotton that had been picked from the nearby fields, and there was a little of it left from last year's harvest. With full bellies, we crawled onto that cotton and went to sleep. Next morning, we got up and went back home.

Some nights, we caught crawdaddies. They were all over the place in the bayous. There were holes in the creek banks, and you could reach down and pull out the crawdaddies. One time, I reached into a hole and pulled out what I thought was a big ol' crawdaddy, but it was a snake! I threw him as far as I could. You only eat the tails of the crawdaddies, which we rolled in corn meal and dropped into the skillet with the boiling grease. Parker did most of the cooking for the group.

The four of us boys did this most Saturday nights through the summer and into fall. When John and Parker turned fifteen, they started drifting off on Saturday nights. They went walking down those dirt roads with their girlfriends. Mug and I just couldn't understand how walking with a girlfriend in the cotton fields at night could be better than being out in the bayou, gigging frogs, catching crawfish and having fun. A couple of years later, we would discover the lure of the girlfriends ourselves, but for now, we were happy just being kids.

About the end of August or early September, the cotton was ready to pick, and we were back in the cotton fields again. We put in about twelve to fourteen hours a day in the fields, and were pulled completely out of school for it. All the cotton was picked by hand. There were no machines around to pick it.

Picking cotton was hard on your hands, back and knees. You carried a cotton sack that was about four feet wide, and could be either ten, twelve or sixteen feet long. It was made of canvas with a tar bottom and a strap to go over your shoulder. Some of the pickers wore knee pads, but I didn't. To pull the cotton out of the boll, you had to slide your fingers between the pod and the fiber, then twist and pull. You used both hands at once and picked two rows at a time. It felt just like picking stickers all day. If your fingers were tough, it didn't bother you as much.

From time to time, you had to grab your sack and shake all the cotton down to the end. Finally, it got so heavy you couldn't pull it any more.

Then you took it to the cotton pen. These were about 150-200 feet apart. They could be an old shack or sharecropper's house. There would be a big two-by-four on the house with a metal scale about three feet long. You had to level the scale by putting a little pear-shaped hooked metal piece called a "pea" on it. The pea would be moved along the scale until the arm leveled, and it would be at the marking showing the weight of the cotton. There was always somebody there to keep track of the numbers, since the pickers got paid based on the pounds of cotton each had picked.

Once there was enough cotton in the pen, they took it to a cotton gin to remove the seeds. They drove the wagon up underneath the gin and a big hose would move around over it and suck the cotton up into the machinery.

After the cotton fiber was separated from the seeds, the fiber was baled, then shipped to a warehouse where the cotton buyers bid on it. A full bale of cotton weighed about 500 pounds or so. At the warehouse, the bale was cut and a small sample pulled out for the buyers to inspect. They stretched it out and examined the fibers, then placed bids on each bale they wanted to buy.

The seed was processed for other uses. Hulls and kernels were separated. The hulls were used for cattle feed, while oil was made from the kernels.

Sometimes on Saturday we went to Clarksdale, about eight miles away. Winfred sold the cotton and gave each of us kids two dollars apiece. It wasn't much money for all the work we'd put in, but Winfred's purpose was not for us to make money. In the time we lived in the delta, we got very little money, clothes or schooling. But in the delta, cotton was king, and everything else came second.

We were not alone in our lack of schooling. The poor Negro children who lived there didn't go to school, either. Sometimes, there were shacks where the small ones had a school set up. But the Negro teachers were not educated enough to teach them much.

I discovered a large, barn-looking house sitting at the forks of two roads. It was being used as a school and a church by the local Negro community. I had missed going to church since I had come to live with Winfred and Lilly. Dad used to make us go every Sunday, but they didn't go to church. Sometimes I would walk down the road to this Negro church after dark on Sundays and sit in the back row to listen to the preacher and sing.

The church had a drummer and a guitar player up front, and when they started singing, everybody went wild. I really enjoyed their music. Sometimes, I knew the songs and would join in. One of my favorites was *Old Time Religion*. Once they started singing a song, it could go on for half an hour, over and over. They prayed a while, then sang a while. I felt like they were really good people. We all pulled together to survive those hard times.

As time passed in the delta, things got worse for us. We worked hard and lots of money was being made. Unfortunately, we never saw any of it. Worst of all, I got cheated out of my sixth and seventh grade school years. Up until then, I'd been doing well in school, and at playing sports.

I was almost thirteen years old by now, and noticed that other children were dressed in nice clothes and shoes. Then I looked at John and myself, and we still wore bib overalls most of the time. With the war on and more people employed, most other people were getting away from wearing overalls and were wearing nice clothes instead. We didn't even have any shoes.

When we went into town this way, we'd see Winfred put all that money from the cotton in his pocket. I never saw him drink, and wondered what he did with all that money. While we were at work in the cotton fields during the day, Winfred disappeared. He always said he had to keep the farm equipment repaired, take the plows to the blacksmith over in Bobo to get them sharpened, have the cultivators repaired, sell the cotton, buy hay and feed for the horses and mules, check on the cottonseed, go to the buyers and find the best one for our cotton. Winfred was always doing these run-around things, and he'd be gone all day long. He only worked in the fields with us maybe one day out of the week.

Many years later, John told me what was really going on. "Joe, you know Winfred was spending all our money on the ladies."

"Oh, he was, huh? So that's what happened to all our hard-earned money. John, how could he be so irresponsible?"

"He had no education and no idea how to handle money, so whenever he got a pocketful of money, he'd spend it. Winfred and Lilly got married when she was fifteen and he was seventeen.

"Really?"

"Oh, yeah. He had no father to keep him straight when he was growing up, and he just wandered around during the Depression."

"He was married to Lilly then?"

"Yep. Lilly let him do whatever he wanted. She never corrected him, and believed everything he said."

"Poor Lilly." I'd always liked my half-sister-in-law.

Even though Lilly was a hard worker—probably more so than any of us—she could not control her husband. After Winfred spent all our money, we had to start working for a plantation owner in our second year in the delta. My half-brother had been renting this property where we were living, and could no longer pay the rent. He decided to put us all to work for one of the big plantation owners in the area.

The arrangement was that we worked for this plantation owner by the hour. I was baling hay, getting $2.50 a day. John was working for the same plantation owner, baling hay, plowing, or whatever needed doing. Even Lilly was working by the week. Winfred came around Saturdays at noon to get our pay from the plantation owner. Even at my age, I knew something was wrong. I was working my ass off, and Winfred was getting all the money.

One day, we were all working in the plantation's cotton field. John, Lilly, the Kaiser family and I were there. Winfred showed up and worked with us for a short time. We were picking cotton, with those long canvas sacks strapped on our backs.

Winfred started complaining, "Joe Abb, you got to work harder."

"Harder?"

"Yeah, harder. You listenin' to me, boy?"

I ignored him.

"Boy, I said you listenin' to me? You answer me when I ask you somethin'. You better start workin' harder and listenin' to what I say."

"Well, then why don't you tell me what you're doin' with all my money?"

"What'd you say to me?"

"I said, what are you doin' with all my money?"

He said, "I'm takin' care of you. Givin' you a place to sleep, feedin' you, buyin' you clothes. Now, shut your damn mouth! I'll take this cotton sack off and beat your ass so bad you ain't gon' be able to walk!"

Everybody in the cotton field got silent for what seemed like about five minutes. They all knew a fight was fixin' to start. Out of all of us, I was the snappy kid that would fight back.

Finally, I yelled, "If you take my money, why can't you send me back to school like all my friends? Buy me some shoes, so I won't have to walk around here barefooted, and get some clothes besides these damned ol' bib overalls with holes all in 'em!" I was crying the whole time I was yelling at Winfred.

Everybody in the cotton field knew I was telling the truth. But the kids only ranged from age 15 to 11, and the rest were women who were so afraid of Winfred they just kept silent.

Winfred knew he could not let this happen; it might spoil his little child-labor scheme. He took off his cotton sack and made a run at me, saying, "You li'l bastard! I done had enough of your shit for one day! When I get through kickin' your ass, there's gonna be more shit in this here cotton field than there is cotton!"

I thought, boy, there's a lot of cotton in this damn field. Winfred and I were working about ten cotton rows apart, so that gave me a head start. I knew he would hurt me really bad if he caught me.

We both moved across that cotton field faster than a John Deere tractor in high gear. He had to stop running to catch his breath, and that was the only time I stopped running. I was younger and had more speed and better wind. As soon as he started running again, so did I. He could not catch me, this I knew.

Our house was three sharecropping houses down the side road from where we were working. I was running for it. When I looked back, all the workers had stopped in the field and were running toward us. I could hear them yelling, "You ain't treatin' that boy right!" and "You oughta be ashamed of yourself! Takin' all his hard-earned money and spendin' it on crazy things. We know what's goin' on with you, Winfred, and you better leave that boy alone!"

Finally, Winfred panted to me, "Tell me what you wanna do, boy. If you stay here, you gonna do what I tell you to do."

Still crying, I yelled back, "I'm gonna leave this damn cotton field and go back to my dad, if I can find him!"

Winfred turned to John and said, "Well, what *you* gon' do, boy?"

John said, "Well, I reckon I'll go with Joe Abb."

So ended my four-year stay with my half-brother, Winfred. John and I left the field together. Mr. Dobbins was the gentleman who owned the plantation where we'd been working. We went to him and asked, "Would you give our pay directly to us instead of Winfred?"

"Well, let's see, here. Let me find y'all in my books." He went to a ledger and found our entries. "Oh, yes. Looks like y'all got two weeks' pay comin' to you." He counted out the bills to us.

"Thank you, suh."

John and I packed our rags in an old cardboard box we got from a country store. We had no suitcases. The two of us hitchhiked from Clarksdale to Pontotoc on Highway 6, almost all the way across the state. Then we made our way down to Bruce. At night it started getting dark and there was no traffic to give us a ride, so we slept by the side of the road, just piled up somewhere in the woods for the night. We arrived in Bruce the next day, about midafternoon.

Chapter 27
Lay-By Time

John and I found our dad living in the old brick jailhouse in Bruce, where the town let him live rent-free. It was the old "calaboose" the police officer had threatened to put me in several years ago for selling peanuts in front of the theater, but it was no longer used as a jail. Dad was none too pleased to see us. He just looked at us for a while, then said, "John. Joe Abb. Why'd y'all come back?" We hadn't seen each other in almost four years.

John and I told him about Winfred's get-rich scheme in the delta, and about how I'd stood up to him. We slept there in the old brick jailhouse with him that night.

Dub was off in the Army now, stationed somewhere in the Philippines. It had been more than three years since he'd left me at Winfred's farm. Dad was way up in his seventies now, and getting his old-age pension of $12 a month, plus an allotment check from Dub of about $50 a month. He was doing pretty well. Since he was born and raised in that area, and was related to a lot of the town, he knew everybody.

We couldn't all stay in the old jailhouse, so Dad called the sheriff to see what he could find for us. John and I slept at the jailhouse some nights, other nights at town's cotton gin.

I got a job setting up pins at the bowling alley. This was done by hand in those days. There were dots on the end of each alley where the pins had to be set up. When a bowler would throw the ball, those pins scattered, and I had to jump up high on a small platform. After the ball came through, I jumped down and spotted the pins again. I also had to retrieve the ball and put it into a wooden rack that rolled it to the other end of the lane by the pull of gravity. I got paid four cents a game, but it went straight to my dad. This went on all evening, until around 10:30. That was about when things closed up in the little town of Bruce.

John got a job working in a creamery. Dad spent his days sitting on the street corner and talking to everybody in the city square. Sometimes, the bowling alley owner would slip a little of my money directly to me. His business was in the same block as the town's café and pool hall. One early morning, I was out behind the building when I noticed a lot of empty pint and half-pint whiskey bottles. There was no legal whiskey in that area in the 1940's, just moonshine. It dawned on me that I could collect those bottles and sell them back to the area bootleggers. Fridays and Saturdays, I made a good amount of cash off the bottles, money that I could actually keep for myself.

Mr. Wash Hughes, who'd given us a room in his boarding house when we'd first moved to Bruce after leaving my mother and her moonshining boyfriend behind, also owned the town's cotton gin. John and I slept in it for a time, where he kept the excess cotton. Somebody had pulled a couple of the vents off around the top of where the cotton was stored, and we'd crawl in there and sleep every night on that cotton. That old brick jailhouse was awfully hot, so this was better. Sometimes the smell of cotton would overwhelm us, and it brought back memories of our time in the delta.

Mr. Hughes eventually let me move out to a shack at his house. I cared for his livestock, and he paid me $10 a week plus my meals. It felt good to work with animals again. That fall, I turned thirteen. Working didn't bother me, but I was getting old enough to want to have control over some of the money I was earning. I was about to find a way to do just that, or so I thought.

🌲
Chapter 28
The Big Adventure

One day at the bowling alley, I overheard some of the sixteen-year-old boys talking about how the federal government was recruiting boys aged sixteen and over to go up to North Dakota and harvest wheat, barley, rye and oats. The government would pay your travel expenses there and back, give you a place to eat and sleep, and pay you sixty cents an hour. Once you got to the Dakotas, however, you had to work ten hours a day. After working for Winfred, that was nothing to me!

The reason the government had to do this was the war. All the young boys were being drafted when they turned eighteen. That left very few men to harvest the wheat fields up in the Dakotas. Sixty cents an hour! Why, that was the highest pay I'd ever heard of.

For the first time in my life, I was making a little bit of money that I actually controlled, and it felt good. When I heard about an opportunity to make more, I had to find a way to join in this wheat harvest.

The group of sixteen-year-olds who hung out at the bowling alley in Bruce included a pair of twins, the Smith brothers, from over in Big Creek. Bo Smith did most of the talking, and he played basketball at the local high school. Neither of them drank or smoked. They were friendly guys, and I hung out with them a lot. Another member of the group was a guy we called "Snag" because he was snaggletoothed. He'd dropped out of school, but I knew him from the school in Pittsboro.

I got with Bo to figure out how I could get in on this wheat harvest deal. He figured out a birthdate for me that would make me just sixteen years old. Over and over again, I went over that date in my head until I could say it with a straight face.

Saturday was the appointed day, and we all met up to go over to Calhoun City to sign up. It was the next town down the road, about ten miles away. The boys lived scattered all over the county. The federal government had set up a pavilion tent in the Calhoun City square to sign up all the young boys to go help with the wheat harvest.

I stepped up and said, "I want to join that wheat harvest."

The agent asked me, "How old are you, boy?"

Without batting an eye, I said, "Sixteen."

"You got a birth certificate?"

"Naw, suh." This was not unusual in rural Mississippi.

He gave me some papers and said, "You get your dad to sign these here papers, and you are on your way to South Dakota."

South Dakota! We'd learned about the different states in school, but I wasn't sure exactly where that was. It was far away from Mississippi, that was all I knew.

We all headed back to Bruce. "What'd they tell you, Joe Abb?" asked Bo.

"He gave me these papers for my dad to sign. Only he ain't gonna sign 'em, I just know it!" I was dejected, thinking I'd never get to go on this great adventure now.

"Well, Joe Abb, we gonna take care of that for you right now. Here, gimme that paper!" said another of the group. He pulled out a pen and signed the paper, then another of my friends affixed his name to it as a witness. And suddenly, I was sixteen years old.

The following Wednesday, I reported back for my journey north for the wheat harvest. The others were as excited as I to be heading north and finding out what lay beyond the state of Mississippi. The Agriculture Department had rented some school buses, and we were put on those and sent over to Grenada.

At Grenada, we were put onto a train, which carried us north. I'd gone for a short train ride to Clarksdale when we lived in the Delta, but this was the first time I'd ridden such a long distance on one. We were assigned seats alphabetically, so we didn't get to sit with our friends. When we got to St. Louis, we had to change trains.

As we got off the train, I was able to find some of my friends and we walked toward the other train together. I kept standing on my tiptoes to look off in the distance as far as I could see. "What you lookin' for, Joe Abb?" said Bo.

"I heard there was supposed to be tall buildings in Saint Louie, so I'm lookin' for 'em."

They all laughed. "Boy, you can't see no tall buildings from here!," said Snag. "You got to get closer into town!"

"Well, how'm I supposed to know that? And how do *you* know that? You ain't never been outside Mississippi, either!" They may have been laughing at me, but they were no more worldly than I was, just a few years older.

It didn't take us long to change trains, then we headed north again. There were no bunks to sleep in, so we all just slept in our seats. The club cars had good food. We each had a meal card on a chain around our necks. The I.D. card—the one saying that I was sixteen years old—hung on a separate chain. I didn't have a penny in my pocket. A thousand miles from home, and flat broke—and I didn't have a worry in the world.

We finally arrived at our destination, a town called Huron, South Dakota. They put us up in a barracks-type building overnight. Early the next morning, we were lined up in front of a building downtown. It looked like the City Hall, or some other kind of public building. There were about five sets of steps out front coming down from the doors of the building.

I could see a good 75 people there to harvest the wheat. Our crowd from Mississippi was in the mix, and also a large number of people with dark skin, darker than ours but not as dark as the Negroes back home. Somebody told me they were Mexicans. The officials started letting the assembled farmers pick their workers. One farmer would pick his five people, then the next, and so on, until we were all chosen.

As each farmer picked his five workers, the size of the crowd kept dwindling. One by one, I said goodbye to my friends from home. At the end, there was only one worker left—me. One farmer pointed at me, laughing, and said, "I don't think you gonna get much work outta that boy at all!" I was three years younger than anybody else there, so I probably did look pretty puny, standing there in my bib overalls.

Finally, a farmer in striped overalls drove up in a 1939 car. He had arrived late, and had to take me because I was the only one left. The farmer was tall, fair in color, and spoke with an accent I'd never heard before. I climbed into the car with him and off we went, out to work the wheat harvest.

Chapter 29
The Harvest

My new boss, as it turned out, was Swedish. His name was Mr. Edvardsson. We drove the twelve miles or so outside of Huron to his farm. All I could see along the way was flat wheat fields. There were no houses, no trees, just wheat. From cotton fields to wheat fields; what a change for me.

When we arrived at the farm, he had a large farmhouse. Most of his sons were in the Army, but one 17-year-old son and his wife lived at the other end of the house from Mr. Edvardsson and his wife. My room was in the back of the house, and they had an indoor toilet. That was something I hadn't experienced much since living in the orphans' home in Jackson; the bus stations had them, but nowhere I'd lived. Just like the ones at the home, it had a chain hanging down from above that you pulled to flush it. There was even electricity in the house, courtesy of a windmill out back.

Mrs. Edvardsson was a big-boned lady with blonde, shoulder-length hair. She always wore house clothes and aprons, and spent most of her time in the kitchen. Both she and her husband were in about their 50's.

"Use de bathroom, den ve vill start vork in de fields," he told me.

I would come to find that the Swedes believe in working all the time, and the same was expected of me. All the farmers in that area were of Swedish, Norwegian and German descent. Mr. Edvardsson took me to a field and showed me how to shock barley by hand. The barley had already been cut and tied in small bundles, and was lying all over the field.

"You pick up de bundles and put dem in dese big shocks," he told me. A shock was a pile of the bundles of barley. It only took him about fifteen minutes to show me how to do it, then he left me alone to work the field.

About one o'clock that afternoon, he showed up with a basked filled with food and water. It was really welcomed, because that field was as hot as any cotton field I'd ever worked. The only difference was in the way you did the work.

The harvest was the hardest work I'd ever done. We worked ten hours a day, and ate four meals a day. After we had shocked all the wheat, barley and rye, we had to take a team of horses and big wagons, load the grain onto them and take it to the center of the field, where there was a stationary combine. With pitchforks, we put the bundles into the combine. It threshed the wheat from the straw. The straw came out one side of it, and the wheat came out the other into a big tank truck.

These horses were the largest I'd ever seen, Clydesdales. They were big roans, and their feet were huge. There were six to eight teams and wagons. The workers were paired off. I worked the left side of the field and my partner worked the right, on the opposite side of the combine. I watched my partner, and whenever he'd head over to the combine, so did I. We both offloaded the wagons into the combine. After offloading, we'd each head back to our sides of the field.

I later learned that everybody had placed bets on whether or not I'd last three days in those fields. My small size in comparison to the other boys had led them to believe that I wouldn't. But with every pitchfork of wheat, I could see that sixty cents an hour, six dollars a day.

There were a lot of small farms in the area, and the farmers would all come over and work on Mr. Edvardsson's farm, then we'd go over and work theirs. It was a real community effort. Every one of them had some kind of a Scandinavian accent. They didn't play around, sing, or do anything except eat, sleep and work. We were all so tired in the evenings, after working all day, that all we did was go home, eat and go to sleep.

After about two weeks, the locals got the idea that I was there to stay. They were surprised at this little guy, coming in there and fighting, but I knew how to work with teams of horses. Everybody liked me and became my friends. Most of the other workers were over forty years old. As a southern child, I'd been taught never to interfere with grownups' conversation, so I really never had much interaction with them outside of work. I mainly listened when they were talking, staying in the background. I laughed when they laughed, and shoveled wheat when they would.

Some of the workers had come from Mexico. They traveled up to work the wheat harvest every year. We would see them off in the distance, working on the next farm over. The land in South Dakota was so flat you could see for miles across those wheat fields. Occasionally, we'd hear the Mexican workers singing songs in Spanish. They always kept their distance from the rest of us, though, and I don't know if they even spoke any English.

We started our days early with a big breakfast. They didn't make biscuits and eggs, like back home. Here, we ate pancakes. Then we'd break for dinner at midday. About four in the afternoon, we'd eat two big sandwiches, then a large evening meal about 6:30. Their diet was heavier than ours back home, and had a lot more meat in it. There was a lot of beef, cheese and soups. I loved all the food, especially those pancakes.

There was a small town about eight or ten miles away. It was smaller than Huron, but I don't recall the name. The town only had about two or three little stores, one of which was a whiskey store. Everybody in our gang had a bottle of booze in their pockets somewhere, except me. They'd go out behind the wagon and have a snort from time to time. I was too young to buy liquor, and never drank it.

On one of our trips into the little town, I asked the owner of the liquor store if he would sell me a bottle because everybody else had one. I wanted to be like the rest of the boys, even though my voice hadn't even changed yet. He said, "No, you're too young."

Finally, everybody went outside the store to get back in the truck to leave. The owner grabbed me by the arm and said, "What do you want?"

I didn't know one whiskey from the other. "Just anything will do," I told him.

"I've got you a pint of apricot brandy."

"That sounds good to me."

I paid him for the brandy and hid the bottle in my pants, just like I'd seen the others do. Going outside, I got in the truck and we headed for the wheat fields. Somehow, having that bottle made me feel equal to the rest of the guys.

Once we got back to the wheat field, I got my team of horses and wagon, got a little away from the others, then turned up that bottle of brandy and took a big gulp. Boy! I started choking and spitting it out. It took me about five minutes to catch my breath. I'd never had anything like that before; only a little bit of beer, but not much. That wine I had made from the possum grapes in the woods near the log cabin wasn't really like whiskey. I thought, "This stuff tastes like crap!" It reminded me of medicine.

Thank goodness, there was nobody around to see me gagging on that brandy. I hid the bottle in the barn and picked it up the next morning to take to the field with me. I started thinking, "Maybe it didn't taste as bad as I thought." After all, everybody else drank, and why would they if it really tasted that bad? About noon, I finally got enough nerve to try and take a small drink. No big gulps this time!

I turned up the bottle and took a very small taste. It was not too bad. From that time on, I always carried my bottle of booze, just like the big boys.

We worked every day until Saturday at noon, when we all headed to Huron for Saturday night. Huron wasn't a big town, except in that part of the country. There was a place that played all the latest swing music. That was all you heard there. There was none of that good country music I liked so much from the Grand Ole Opry; they didn't get that show on the radio up in South Dakota.

I had no idea what month it was. The weather was still hot, or at least it felt that way in those fields every day. I always did whatever my boss told me to do, so I was a good worker. On Saturdays, he would give me six dollars to spend Saturday night, keeping the rest of my money until I'd stayed the allotted time.

Mr. Edvardsson told me, "I vill send yer money home ven de job is over, and I vill give you enough to get home on. You are too young to have dis kind of money."

Truthfully, I didn't know how much money I really made. I never asked anybody else what they were getting, just worked and got my money to spend Saturday night. I trusted Mr. Edvardsson, and his keeping it was okay with me. He'd spotted my being so young early on, and looking back, he actually took my hand and helped me through the harvest. He had my dad's address in Mississippi, and something told me he'd written to him and had found out all about me.

Finally, the long, hot days in the wheat field were over for me. I had completed my required time working the wheat harvest. I had surprised them all, and stayed the required time. If you didn't stay and work that long, the government wouldn't pay your way home, so I really didn't have any options. At the end of my time there, my boss said, "Let's go to Huron and get you some decent clothes."

He and his wife went with me to a clothing store in Huron. This was unusual, because she never went to town. They bought me some shoes, shirts, and trousers, really nice things. Of course, it was paid for with my money.

"You know, Joe Abb, if you vant to, you can stay vith us and go to school here in Sout' Dakota," they told me.

"Thanks, but I think I'll go back to Miss-sippi." Mississippi was home to me. I'd fallen in love with Pittsboro when I was younger, and that was home. Mississippi was really the only place I'd ever been, and it just felt like home.

The Edvardssons dressed me up in some of my new clothes and gave me some cash for the long trip back to Mississippi. They drove me to Huron to meet the train home. As I boarded, both of them hugged my neck and wished me the best of luck. There was even a tear in Mrs. Edvardsson's eye. It had never dawned on me that they had any feelings for me.

When I got on the train, to my surprise, there was only one other boy who had signed up with me in Calhoun County, Mississippi who had stayed the whole time. He was one of the boys I didn't know too well, but he was from a poor family, like me. The work was too hard for all the other boys, and their mothers had sent them money to return home after about three weeks. Meanwhile, this little runt of a boy—or so they had thought—had outworked all the rest of them. I settled into my seat for the long ride south.

Chapter 30
Return to the Delta

The trip to Grenada, Mississippi from Huron, South Dakota took two days and one night. When the train arrived, I hitchhiked the fifteen miles back to Bruce.

Upon arrival in Bruce, I looked up my dad. "I'd like to have that money my boss sent to you from South Dakota to keep for me."

"You can't have that kind of money," he told me.

"Why not? It's my money. I worked my ass off in them fields to get that money!"

I'd returned to more of the same. More of people keeping away from me the money that I'd earned.

One day, my dad received a letter from Winfred. He was still working in the delta, and asked for me to return. What's more, he promised to pay me at noon every Saturday for picking cotton, not like when I was there before.

Dad finally agreed to give me some of my money to return to the delta to pick cotton with Winfred and Lilly. I'd turned fourteen in October, and this time they treated me well. Despite Winfred's mismanagement of their finances, they were still hanging onto the farm. The cotton crop they had was ready to produce, but they were about to get thrown off the land. They'd gotten far behind in the harvest, and the cotton was falling out of the bolls onto the ground. Cotton was lying all over the place, with nobody to pick it.

By working long hours, we were able to save most of the cotton crop, and I got paid every Saturday at noon. If nothing else, South Dakota had taught me to pay as you go, put your money in your pocket and don't let anybody else handle it for you. Winfred sold the cotton as fast as he could. He never paid the landowner rent on the farm, keeping all the money for himself. He sold all his farm equipment, along with the horses and mules, then skipped town on the landowner.

Even my beloved Nell was sent to a plantation called The Village. With the war going on, tractors weren't being manufactured, so all the plowing was being done with horses and mules. John told me he went by there many years later and saw Nell out in the pasture. She was the only horse among many mules in the pasture. John whistled, and she came over to him and nuzzled him.

It was Christmastime of 1945. All the cotton was picked. I had a lot of money, and there was no more to be made there in the delta. This had been the first year I had not gone to school any time, all year. I would have been in the eighth grade, had I not missed so much for the past few years.

Returning to my dad at Bruce, I found him healthy, still living in that old, one-room brick jailhouse. He was in his high seventies now, and had some problems getting around from his old injury.

The Murphy family let me move in with them and start back to school at Pittsboro. I'd missed the first four months of the eighth grade, and was far behind the other students. Most of the kids I'd started first grade with, years before, were still there. A lot of them came from families who made them go to school every day. My dad had been that way, but nobody else in my family seemed to value education the way he did.

I was so far behind that it was embarrassing when the teacher would call on me to read. I missed every other word and the kids would just stare at me. The kids who used to know me couldn't believe I was that dumb. It wasn't a matter of being dumb, just having missed half a year of school. When I'd been there before, I was one of the smartest kids in school, but now it felt like I'd never catch up. Turned out this would be the last schooling I'd have for a while.

Chapter 31
Winds of Change

The struggle to catch up in school was too much for me, and I quit soon after starting. I worked around different farms and any place I could find work, sleeping in the old jail with Dad at night. He was a strange person, but he always let me in his place at night. At least it kept the rain and bugs off me.

John had gone off to work for a farmer a few miles outside of town. I didn't see him for a while. One Saturday, he came into town around noon. "That farmer treats me pretty darn good, Joe Abb" he told me.

"That's good, John."

"Yes-s-suh. He give me five acres of cotton if I help him work the rest of the farm. All the money made on them five acres is *mine*."

"That's a good deal. Just make sure he really pays you." I'd learned my lessons from all those years of harvesting cotton and wheat for next to nothing.

I started seeing John regularly on Saturdays after that, always around noon.

The pool hall in Bruce was a big hangout for teenage boys. It was not very big, and was in back of a café. They sold bootlegged whiskey back there, too. The café had fly paper hanging up all over the place to catch the hordes of flies that always seemed to be around in Mississippi. The screen doors had holes in them, and were pretty much useless. Every time you looked up when you were eating there, you'd think one of those flies was going to fall off into your soup or onto your hamburger. You'd see the flies get stuck and try to wiggle their way off the paper, but they stayed on. They were so thick the owner had to change that fly paper every day. I'd never really paid attention to it before, but all the cafés in the south in the 1940's had the same thing.

One Saturday, I was hanging out at the pool hall when Bo Smith came in from Big Creek. He was the one who'd figured out my fake birthday to qualify me for the wheat harvest. I'd always liked Bo.

"Hey, Bo! How you doin'?"

"All right, Joe Abb. What you doin'?"

"Aw, just hangin' out."

136

"You still got your I.D. card from that wheat harvest?"

"Well, yeah, Bo. It's right here, round my neck." I was still wearing my I.D. card on the same chain around my neck.

"Man, that was something, that trip up north."

"Yeah, sure was. 'Cept I heard most of y'all didn't make it the whole time."

"Naw," he laughed. "That sun up there was too hot for me. Momma sent us the money to get home."

"You just ain't worked long enough in them cotton fields, that's all it is."

"I reckon."

Several other boys were with Bo who had also made the trip up to South Dakota. We all drank Cokes, ate hamburgers and played pool for ten cents a game. It was nice to have some money of my own that I actually had control over.

Before the day was over, about eight guys from the wheat harvest had shown up. None of them had done their full time there, but they'd gone along at first. All of them had just turned eighteen, or were just about to. The Army had sent them draft notices to report for duty in three weeks. Even though the war was over, the service was still drafting eighteen-year-old boys. There was still a lot of work to be done.

"I don't wanna be in no Army," said one.

"Naw, man, that's just the grunts. They get sent in to do the worst work."

"I think we oughta all join the Navy instead."

"Yeah, that sounds good to me. Them Navy guys, they get all the girls."

"I dunno, though, what about havin' to be out at sea on one of them big ships? I don't know if I could do that. What if the ship gets sunk? I can't swim too good."

"Naw, dummy, the war's over. Ain't nobody sinkin' ships now."

"That's right, after we done showed them Japs who was boss."

"Still, though, I don't think I could do that, on them ships. I'm just goin' in the Army."

"Well, alright, y'all all do whatever you want, but I'm gon' sign up for the Navy."

"Where you got to go to do that?"

"They got a Navy recruitin' station over in Grenada. In the post office there."

By the time the conversation was over, most of the others had decided to join the Navy, too. Two had even opted for the Marine Corps.

We left the café, everyone heading back toward their homes. "Alright, then, we all gon' meet up here tomorrow an' go over to Grenada to sign up for the Navy."

"Alright. That sounds good to me."

I went back to the old town jail to sleep, and decided to go with them to Grenada. Even if I was too young to join up, it was something interesting to do. The Navy had always fascinated me, ever since I'd seen that sailor at my school, just after the war had broken out. If I went with them, I could find out what I'd have to do to get in when I was old enough. It was a big deal in those days, for a boy to go into the Navy. Most all the boys in our county went into the Army. I dreamed that night of sailing the oceans, dressed in one of those fancy uniforms with the thirteen buttons on the pants.

Chapter 32
Too Young?

Next morning, I was the first boy on the street. The jailhouse was just behind the pool hall, and with my farm background, I was trained to get up at daybreak. Those of us who lived in Bruce were meeting about four doors down from the pool hall, at another little café. It was where we all hung around to play pinball whenever we weren't in the pool hall.

It was after eight when the other guys started to show up for the trip to Grenada. By nine, they were all there except the Smith boys from Big Creek. They were going to meet us there. All in all, there were about fifteen of us. We all had breakfast and drank plenty of coffee, then started our trip.

We already had a ride to Calhoun City, which was about half the distance there. I don't think there was a car in the whole county, so we were riding in log trucks, dump trucks, pickup trucks, chicken trucks, milk trucks—whatever would give us a ride. Most of the people in the café having breakfast were going that way, anyway, and they'd let you ride with them because you were going into the military. It was an honor for them to give you a ride. Everybody was very kind to people who were going to fight for our country.

Most of us got off at Calhoun City and walked down the road to Highway 8, which went to Grenada. Everything was in Grenada because of the railroad that ran through there, heading toward Memphis to the north and New Orleans to the south. That made the town the center of everything around there. Grenada had a big post office with a Navy recruiting station in it.

We arrived in Grenada about 11:30 in the morning, and made our way to the recruiting station. Bo did all the talking for the group. He was the one with the big mouth, and he was trying to sell the Chief Petty Officer on everyone in the group.

That CPO was a sharp guy, to me. He had ribbons on his uniform, and his shoes were shiny as they could be. His uniform wasn't like the sailor's uniform I'd seen before, it looked more like an Army uniform. I guessed that was how the officers dressed. He looked to be in about his late twenties or early thirties, and was just under six feet tall. When he spoke, it was with distinction.

The chief let Bo talk about how good these guys were. Then he said, "I think I can get you boys out of the Army and into the Navy. That'll take some doing, but I think I might be able to work that out, as long as you have not actually been sworn into the Army."

"Nawsuh, we ain't done that yet," said Bo.

"Well, first of all, you need to be able to swim and be able to read and write at a seventh-grade level."

"Yessuh. We done finished high school, most of us."

"All right. Here are some forms you need to fill out. They ask about how far you went in school, and all that."

I was sitting in the back of the office, listening to everything he said. Even though I was too young to join, I played the game and listened to the chief just like the other boys.

"If y'all stay in the Navy for twenty years, you'll get a good retirement. You'll also get medical care for the rest of your lives, and all the other benefits of being in the Navy."

"Hell, chief, I just want not to get in the Army!" one of the guys piped in. "Do my time in the Navy and get the hell out. I ain't no lifer, so what's the shortest time I can sign up for and get the hell out?"

"Well, we have a new program where you boys can sign up for two years and then go home if you want."

"That sounds good to me," said Bo. All the others agreed.

Then the chief said, "All you boys line up in a single line." He made each of them read a sheet of paper that was equivalent to a seventh-grade reading level. None had any problems with it, or with doing the math he made them do. Next, he gave them an eye test and told them, "When you get down to Jackson, you will get a full examination. So if you can't see, hear, or anything, they will take you out, but the Army will still take you. I just have to check on some of the basic things here, before you get to Jackson. All I need to know today is, number one, can you see lightning?"

"Yessuh," they all answered.

"Good. Number two, can you hear thunder?"

"Yessuh," again in unison.

"And, number three, can all you guys fart?"

There was a long pause, then laughter. They all said, "Yessuh! Sho' can, suh!"

One of the guys said, "I can understand, if you can see lightning, that means you can see. If you can hear thunder, that means your ears is alright. But what's this fartin' thing got to do with my health?"

The chief said, "Boy, if you can fart good, your insides are alright, so just step aside and you'll be in uniform in a few minutes."

He took up all their paperwork and said, "Now, I'll let all the doctors down in the big recruiting place in Jackson do the rest of the physical. I want all you guys to be back here next Wednesday, ready to leave for Jackson."

They had already signed their papers, even though they wouldn't be sworn in until they got down to Jackson.

The chief continued, "And if you pass your physical examination, you will all be going on to boot camp either on the West Coast or the East Coast."

"Alright, suh. We gon' be here," said Bo. "C'mon, boys, let's get over to the bus station and get us somethin' to eat."

They all left the post office building and headed over to the Greyhound bus station. I was still sitting all the way in the back of the recruiting station as they headed for the door, watching and listening to the show. As the last of them walked out, the chief said to me, "Why didn't you join the Navy with your friends?"

"Aw, I'm too young, suh."

"How old are you?"

"Only seventeen." It wasn't true, but my U.S. Department of Agriculture I.D. from the wheat harvest said that it was.

"Son, you can join if you're seventeen, with your parents' permission and signature. Do you have a birth certificate?"

"Naw suh, but I do have this official federal I.D. card." I showed him my wheat harvest I.D., which was still hanging around my neck.

He looked it over and said, "This will do. I can get you in the Navy. And just in the short time I've been talking to you, by God, I think you might even be an Admiral before you get out!"

That chief was no slouch in recruiting. My eyes flickered. I didn't even know what an admiral was, but I knew it was something. So I filled out all the same papers as the other guys, and passed all the tests. Then the chief said, "You go on home now, and talk to your mother."

My face fell at that. "I ain't got no momma," I told him. Well, I did somewhere, but I hadn't seen her for eight years. By this time, I'd given up longing for her.

He said, "Well, then talk to your father, and get him to sign. Everywhere the Navy goes is a paradise, every meal is a banquet, and every day is like a holiday. And, of course, you'll have the prettiest girls in the world."

That really excited me. I thought this chief must know everything.

"All right, I'll talk to my dad."

"If he signs these papers, come back Wednesday and I'll put you in the Navy."

I made my way over to the Greyhound station and met up with the other boys.

"Where you been, Joe Abb?"

"I been talkin' with that Navy chief," I said. "He says he can get me in the Navy!"

"Naw! No kiddin'! You're only fourteen!"

"I know, but I still got this I.D. card from the wheat harvest. You remember we had to tell 'em I was older to get me into that."

"That's right! Dammit all, Joe, if you ain't goin' in the Navy with us!"

We finished our lunches and headed back home. Some went on back to Bruce, while others split up and went to their homes, knowing either the Army or the Navy was going to get them within two weeks. I left them behind me and headed back to the old jailhouse, still wondering how I was going to get my father to sign those papers.

Chapter 33
Commitment

When I got back to Bruce, Dad was lying on his cot in the old jail-house. I gave him the papers to sign and he said, "Naw, I been in the state penitentiary once, and if I sign those papers and get caught, I'll be back in the pen."

"Dad, you're way, way up in your seventies now. If you sign these papers, I'll make you out an allotment, and Uncle Sam'll give you $50 a month. You'll live like a king. I'll put you down as a dependent."

"Let me think about it for a couple of days."

Dad went to the mayor of Bruce and talked with him for some time. I think the mayor may even have been his distant kin. Bruce was such a small town that the mayor really didn't have much responsibility.

The mayor said, "Bill, I'll sign to witness your signature, and that'll do the job. I think that boy should go off into the Navy. You're too old to take care of yourself, much less take care of that young boy. The city done give you that ol' brick jailhouse to live in, or you'd be in the poorhouse. So the best we can do is put that boy in the Navy. At least he'll get three meals a day and some new clothes to wear.

"You know, he is a fine young boy, and a very hard worker. If he stays in this hay-shakin' town, I will guarantee you, he's gon' wind up becomin' a damn moonshiner. 'Cause that's where the money is, and he's smart enough to know that. So, Bill, send his ass off with the U.S. Navy. He's gon' make a good sailor. Besides, that's what he wants to do."

Dad agreed to sign the papers, and the mayor witnessed his signature.

Now, I had five days to report back to the post office in Grenada, where that Navy chief would be waiting for me. The time passed slowly. I played pool every day and hung out at the pool hall, talking to my friends.

"Lawd, Joe Abb, you gon' join the Navy?" said one who was my age.

"Yeah, my dad done signed the papers, and everything."

"Man, that's great! I sho' wish I could pull off somethin' like that myself."

Back in the middle of the woods in Mississippi, going in the Navy was a big deal.

Finally, Wednesday morning dawned. I didn't have a suitcase for traveling, so I went to the town's grocery store and got a box to put my belongings in. It said "MILES SALT" in big, red letters on the side. Not that I had much—just an old pair of shoes with holes in them, a spare set of underwear, an extra pair of socks and an extra shirt. I put all my things in that Miles Salt box, tied a rope around it and headed for Grenada.

My best clothes, I put on to wear until I got issued a sailor suit. The best I had was a nice shirt and a pair of bib overalls. I set out hitchhiking toward Grenada. None of the other boys who had gone with me to sign up ever showed. They were supposed to report back that day, too, and I didn't know what had happened to them. But I couldn't wait around; I had an appointment to keep!

My first ride took me about four miles, to Pittsboro, where I'd gone to grade school. There were some boys about seventeen years old standing in front of Calhoun County's small courthouse. I knew them all. They started laughing and pointing, and one of them said, "Joe Abb, where you goin' with that Miles Salt box?"

"I'm goin' to the U.S. Navy for two years."

"Lawd, boy, they gon' laugh you off that ship, with that Miles Salt box for a suitcase!"

They were just having fun, so I laughed it off, but I suppose I did look kind of silly carrying that salt box with the plow rope tied around it.

I joked around with them in front of the courthouse until I got my next ride, to Calhoun City. A pickup truck that was going that way came along, and I jumped in the back with my Miles Salt box and all the rags I had inside it. We headed down Highway 9 to Calhoun City.

The driver turned to me and said, "Where you goin' big boy, with that Miles long salt box?"

"All my clothes're in this box, and I'm goin' to Grenada to join the Navy."

"You look like you might be a mite young to be goin' off to war. Besides, if they take you, they gon' throw that Miles Salt box in the ocean and put a purty li'l boy blue sailor suit on you with one of them funny little white hats on your head!"

It's true that the Navy uniform was kind of strange, but all the girls went wild over it. The driver continued, "I was a World War One veteran, and I was a soldier. Those damn sailors always stole my woman, for some reason."

We talked the whole trip to Calhoun City. As he dropped me off there, he shouted back, "Good luck to you, and I hope you like the Navy better'n I liked the damn Army!"

"Thank you, suh!"

Next, I needed to head west on Highway 8, the last leg of my trip to

Grenada. Sticking out my thumb, I immediately got a ride headed there. This driver was also curious about my "suitcase."

"Boy, what you got in that there Miles Salt box?"

"Aw, it's just my clothes."

"Where you goin', with all your clothes in that box?"

"I'm goin' to Grenada to join the U.S. Navy."

"Well, boy, you ain't gon' need nothin' in that big ol' Miles Salt box. The Navy's gon' throw away all them rags you call clothes, them plow shoes with holes in 'em, and give you all new stuff. They gon' feed you and give you a paycheck every month."

"Every month? I heard the Navy pays every two weeks."

"How 'bout that! In the Army, we only got paid once't a month. Gon' get paid ever' two weeks, and you gon' get to meet all the girls all over the world. Hell, all I ever saw was them mud trenches in France and Germany. I wish I'd done gone in the Navy. But, hell, that's more'n twenty years ago. That's in the past."

He let me out by the Greyhound bus station in Grenada. The post office was just behind it. It was about noon, and there was nobody in the recruiting station. It was locked up. Here I was, having spent most of my money, and I was expecting the Navy to feed me and put me up for the night. That was what the chief had told me, that the Navy would pay for everything as of noon that day.

Leaving my box in the old bus station, I walked around Grenada. About 1:30, I went back to the post office, hoping the chief would be there. I set my box of rags down at the recruiting office door and waited. Everybody who passed was looking at me and laughing at me, sitting there with that old Miles Salt box all tied up with a rope.

About 2:30, the chief recruiter finally showed up. He was driving a wooden station wagon that had "U.S. NAVY RECRUITER" in big letters on the side. He said, "How long you been waiting?" I thought he must be from Jackson, he spoke so refined and well-mannered.

"Aw, 'bout two hours."

"Where are all the other guys?"

"I'm th'only one come back."

"Those bastards had better show tomorrow, or I'll call the Army and they'll take care of 'em. We don't need people like that in the Navy. Boy, if you say you're gonna be here, you'd better be here."

He kind of scared me a little. I said, "Yessuh, I'm here."

The chief had a passenger with him in the station wagon. She was a beautiful blonde in her mid-twenties. I thought she looked like a movie star. She had on a Hollywood-type suit and plenty of makeup. Church folks in the south didn't wear makeup like that back then. I could not take my eyes off her, even though I assumed she was his wife. She had the prettiest smile I had ever seen. The lady was really nice, too.

That recruiter could see how fascinated I was with his girl, and she played along. "I know you're going to love the Navy," she said. "Once you get in, you're going to be very happy." I could tell she wasn't from the south. She both looked and sounded like the ladies I'd seen in the movies.

She went inside the post office and the chief opened the back door of the station wagon so I could put my Miles Salt box in it. He winked at me and said, "Hey, boy, when you put that sailor suit on, you gon' have girls like that followin' you around all over the place!"

That just made me quiver. "Boy, that's the prettiest lady I ever saw!"

"Yup. You might be right. I kinda like her myself."

We waited around the recruiting station a while longer and none of the other boys ever showed up. "Well, we better get on down the road," said the chief. "We got a two-hour drive down to Jackson, and we got to get this sailor there!"

The three of us got into the station wagon, me in the back seat. The pretty blonde talked to me about my young life. "Have you ever been in Jackson before?"

"Yes'm, I lived there for two years."

"Oh, really? Where?"

"At the big orphans' home."

There was a long pause, then she said, "You don't have a mother or father?"

"Well, yes'm, but it's a long story. When I get out of the Navy in twenty years, I'm gon' tell you all about it. See, one day, I'm gon' write a big, fat book about my life, goin' back to the days when they put me in that orphans' home. I think I'll end the book when I join the Navy."

"Are you gonna put me in your book?"

"Yes ma'am—that is, if the chief don't mind."

The chief said, "You have my permission to put her in your book. You can't say anything bad about this young lady, now."

"Naw suh, I would never, never say nothin' bad about her. I'll just say she's the prettiest lady I ever saw."

She said, "When you get a little older and become an officer in the Navy, you come back, and I'll ditch this ol' dirty chief and run away with you!"

They both laughed, then she said, "Boy, you're going to make a great bullshittin' sailor! I don't think you're going to have any problems making it in the Navy. But what you ought to do is get you an education in the Navy. You can finish high school and take some college courses. As young as you are, you can make it."

146

The chief said, "If you're going to write anything about me, just take that page out and wipe your butt on it. That will make both you and me happy."

He started laughing and said, "Well, we're coming into the city limits of Jackson now."

It was starting to get dark, and the city lights were on. I'd seen these lights many years ago, that time I'd run away from the orphanage. But this time, I got to see much more of the city. Jackson was the biggest city I'd ever seen, even on my trip to South Dakota. There were tall buildings that I counted twelve floors in. The state capitol looked just like the White House to me, only smaller.

The chief parked the wooden station wagon outside a large hotel on Main Street. He said, "This is as far as I can take you. You're on your own from here on."

He gave me a handful of tickets that looked like the ones they used to use at the movie theater in Bruce. Handing me two big, brown envelopes, he said, "Go through that door and give the man behind the desk this envelope. This will take care of your lodging and eating until they ship you out to your boot camp. The other envelope, you need to take to the capitol building to room 240 tomorrow. Just drop it off, then come back here and report to the front desk."

"Yessuh. Thank you, suh." I got out of the station wagon, got my Miles Salt box out of the back and started inside the hotel. The beautiful blonde lady looked at me. I think she could tell I was too young to be joining the Navy. She put one arm around me and said, "Good luck, Joe. I think you'll enjoy the Navy."

"Thank you, ma'am."

I turned and walked into the hotel. That was the last time I ever saw her or the recruiting chief.

🌲
Chapter 34
All Grown Up

The hotel was one of the biggest and best in Jackson. During the war, the government had taken it over for the draft, to house new draftees and recruits. The lobby looked elegant, with nice carpet and furniture. The desk was straight ahead, slightly to the right, across the lobby.

I walked over to the desk. The man behind it was middle aged, and looked at me like he was thinking, "Well, what do we have here?" There I stood, grimy from the trip, in my overalls and shirt, carrying that Miles Salt box tied together with a plow rope. Those big, red, box-car letters on it clearly read, "BUY MILES SALT."

He finally spoke to me. "Man, I been here all during World War Two, checkin' these people in, these draftees and volunteers, and after all this time, you take the cake. Most everybody that's come through here either had a suitcase or a handbag. Some of 'em didn't even have nothin'. But you the only one showed up with a red-lettered Miles Salt box, with a damn big plow rope tied around the damn thing. What in hell you got in that box that's so important?"

"Everything I own's in this box," I told him. "All my clothes and belongin's. That's why I tied the plow rope around it, so it wouldn't pop open and lose somethin'."

"You ain't embarrassed, luggin' that box across the state of Miss'sippi?"

"Naw, suh, 'cause I ain't never owned no suitcase. It don't bother me none."

"You have more guts than anybody that's ever come through this station."

It never occurred to me that any of these people commenting on my Miles Salt box were making fun of me. But it must have elicited sympathy from the desk clerk. He gave me a room key and some extra meal tickets. "Go down the street to that little café," he said. "and eat all you want. My wife owns that café, and I'm in charge of givin' out all these military meal tickets."

The tickets he gave me were different from the ones I'd gotten from the chief. I took them and started out the door.

"Here. Gimme that Miles Salt box, and I'll stash it back here for you."

"Alright. Thank you, suh."

"And bring me some food back, you hear?" he called after me.

"Alright, suh."

I walked down the street and found his wife's café. After eating everything I could hold, I gave his wife a handful of the meal tickets, keeping some for the next day. "Can you fix some food to go for the desk clerk at the hotel? He asked me to bring him back something."

"We sho' can." The waitress went back behind the counter and put together his food. She didn't charge me anything for it, since it was for the proprietor's husband, and I'd given her way more meal tickets than I'd needed to, anyway.

The owner came out and handed me a sackful of food, which I took back to the clerk in the hotel lobby.

"Here's your food, suh. Can I have my box back?"

"Okay; here's your box, boy. I still don't know why you're luggin' that stuff with you."

"It's all I've got in the world, suh. Thank you." Then I went up to my room to sleep.

The room wasn't like a regular hotel room. The government had come in and taken out all the usual hotel furniture, replacing it with their own military-issue things. It had four cots, three of which were already occupied. I took the empty one, removed my holey shoes, laid down with all my clothes on, and quickly fell asleep.

Next morning, I was supposed to take the big, brown envelope over to the state capitol after eight o'clock and leave it at that room number the chief had given me. I got up early, as usual, and walked out on Main Street. Going back to the same café, I ate two breakfasts, paying with another handful of those military meal tickets. The café owner and her husband were making a lot of money by having him hand out the tickets for her place.

Afterward, I headed for the capitol building, which you could see at the end of the main street. It was about ten blocks away. When I got there, something made me nervous as hell. There were at least fifty steps going straight up to the entrance with the door. I'd never looked inside the envelope, but something told me that it contained a letter to confirm my true birth date by asking for my birth certificate. There was a large trash can in front of the steps. I walked over and dropped the envelope into it.

That taken care of, I walked back to the hotel for my physical exam. We were all supposed to meet in the basement of the building about nine o'clock with the other big envelope to hand over to the medical personnel.

As I entered the room, all I could see were rows of benches and about a hundred men standing around naked. One of the men said to me, "Boy, gitcher britches off and join the crowd!" I did as I was told.

It didn't look like there were any military personnel around. All the doctors and medical personnel must have been civilians. They were all wearing white smocks. They gave us the regular physical—eyes, ears, nose, and we even had to bend over and get the old "finger-wave". This physical was for the Navy and Marines, and was a little stricter than the Army physical.

Next, they had us all stand up on the benches, buck naked. One of the doctors announced, "We're going to check to see if any of you have a venereal disease."

I turned to the guy standing next to me on the bench and asked, "What's a vener-al disease?"

"That's what happens when you mess around with the women. Makes your penis sore, and makes it drip. What the doctor will do is milk your penis down, just like milkin' a cow. If anything comes out, you might have a vener-al disease, or somethin' else, and you might not even get in the Navy...but I think the Army will still take you," he laughed.

Down the line came the doctor, and I was scared to death. I was only fourteen years old, and had never been exposed to women. Watching the others standing on the bench, I figured out that when he came to me, I was supposed to reach up with my thumb and finger and pull down on my penis, then he would check to see if there was anything coming out. At fourteen, I had very little pubic hair. All the others were men, and the difference was obvious.

When the doctor got to me, he looked down at my penis, then looked at me again. He shook his head and said, "Boy, have you ever messed with any women?"

The question scared me to death. I screamed, "Naw, suh! Naw, suh! I ain't never messed with no women!"

He said, "Okay," then moved on down the line to the next guy. The next doctor looked at me and winked. "Son, you're startin' a new life in the Navy. You'll know all about it in a couple of years." That was the end of my venereal check for the Navy.

We were all glad when the physical exam was over. Each of us went our own way, either back to the rooms, or walking around Jackson; some had lunch. I was never shy, but for some reason I just kept to myself and didn't try to make any friends here. There was so much going on, and there really wasn't a lot of time to talk to anybody. We had a few hours before we had to be back in the hotel basement to find out where we were going for basic training.

After our evening meal, we reassembled in the basement. One by one, our names were called and a city given that was where we were to go. I waited to hear my name, and it was finally shouted out: "Overby, Joseph"

"Here," I said, as I'd observed the others doing.

"Norfolk, Virginia."

I'd never heard of Norfolk before, but that was where I was going. When all the names had been called, they announced, "Okay, everybody going to Norfolk, get in the corner over there. If you're going to San Diego, California, get over in that corner. Great Lakes, Illinois, over there. Marines, get over in that fourth corner to go to Parris Island." Everybody shuffled off to their allotted corners, like a bunch of school children finding their classes for the first time.

The smartest, biggest, meanest guys were chosen to take the orders for each of the groups. I don't think they were enlistees, because they were dressed as civilians. Our guy called the roll again for everyone in the group, then gave us each several meal tickets. After that, we all got on a bus and were taken to the train station. The drive was only about five or six blocks.

The station was nice; Jackson had a population of about 150,000 at the time, so it was the biggest city in the state. There were so many people there. Most of them were dressed very nicely, not like me. I had holes in my shoes, and had been wearing the same clothes for at least two days. To top it all off, I was still carrying that Miles Salt box on my shoulder. Most people at the station had suitcases.

As I walked to the train, I noticed people staring at me, and could not understand why. Some would just smile and speak to me. They could tell I was just a dumb kid that came from nowhere and didn't know any better.

I finally got on board the train, putting my Miles Salt box in the storage bin over my seat. Nobody else seemed as excited as me, but I just couldn't wait to get to Norfolk and be in the Navy. The train started to roll, and we were on our way.

Chapter 35
New Shoes

Sitting next to me on the train was an Army draftee. That train was filled with people going into the military. A lot of them already had uniforms on. I talked to my neighbor a while, and he finally said, "I wish I'd have joined the Navy instead of the Army."

From time to time, the man in charge of our group would come through to check on us. Before long, I fell asleep. When I woke up, it was with two Shore Patrolmen (SP's) shaking me. Scared me to death! I thought they had found out about my birth certificate, and were going to send me back to Bruce.

"Wake up, boy!" one of them said sternly. "You got to change trains here."

"Where are we?" I asked.

"Atlanta, Georgia."

I'd never been to Georgia before. "What time is it?"

"Five a.m. Now get to hell up from here and get your ass on your train."

I got up and pulled that Miles Salt box off the rack, putting it back on my shoulder. All the other passengers stopped what they were doing to watch. Everything I had was in that box, and I was not going to leave it behind. It was a little chilly outside on the platform, but not all that much different from Jackson. Good thing, since I had no coat. I followed the other Navy recruits through the terminal.

I'd thought the terminal in Jackson was nice, but the Atlanta one was the prettiest building I'd ever seen. It had marble floors and everything. I kept staring; I'd never seen anything like this before! We made our way over to the platform for the train that would take us the rest of the way to Norfolk. I don't remember seeing the guy who'd been in charge of our group after this.

It wasn't long before the train was on its way. I went back to sleep, and woke up to eat breakfast around seven a.m. It was still dark outside the train My clothes were starting to get a little smelly. After breakfast, I went back to my seat and waited for the sun to come up.

Around daylight, the train finally pulled into the Portsmouth, Virginia railroad station. It was just across the river from Norfolk, and there was no bridge crossing the river between the two at that time. There were about fifty SP's there to meet the trains. They directed us to several large, haze-gray buses that said "U.S. NAVY" across the sides.

Virginia was a lot colder than Georgia, so I untied the plow rope around my Miles Salt box and pulled out my extra shirt. It was all I had to put on to keep warm.

We were loaded aboard the buses, which immediately pulled out onto High Street, the main street of Portsmouth. At the end of the street were several ferry slips. I had never seen so many ferry boats in my life. As a matter of fact, I had never seen one at all, not even when I had lived in the delta.

Each ferry carried about ten of the large buses. As we were ferried across the Elizabeth River, I got my first glimpse of a large body of salt water, with all kinds of ships going up and down. Tugboats, barges and everything. Even though I'd stood on the banks of the Mighty Mississip' as a child, and had seen some barges and tugboats, I'd never seen anything like this. All these huge ships were passing within 150 feet of each other. It was hard for me to contain my excitement, watching all this from my seat on the bus aboard the ferry.

It took less than twenty minutes to cross the river from Portsmouth to Norfolk. The ferry boats would unload the full buses, reload with empty ones and head back across, one after the other. They did it really fast, too.

The bus moved through downtown Norfolk and headed toward the big Navy base. At that time, Norfolk was the largest Navy base in the world. Occasionally, we could catch glimpses of the Elizabeth River, and parts of the Hampton Roads Bay. My eyes got bigger as I thought, "How big *is* this thing called ocean?" I never thought there was that much water in the world, and I still hadn't even seen the Chesapeake Bay. This was sure a long way from those muddy cow ponds I used to swim in as a child. All during the ride, I kept to myself and didn't talk to anyone else. All I could do was stare at all that water and be thrilled to death.

About 45 minutes to an hour later, we arrived at the base. The buses pulled through a large gate. At the gate stood Marines with rifles and guns. Boy, it was exciting for me to see that! Beyond the gates, it was all sailors. Everybody had a rifle on their shoulder and had these old boot leggings on their legs.

Our bus stopped. The driver opened the door and a petty officer who was to be our company commander stepped onto the bus. He looked like he was going to shoot everybody on there. Atop his head was a white hat. He had three chevrons, which I didn't understand the significance of at that time. There were hash marks on his sleeve, too. After looking us all over for a moment, he finally spoke.

"My name is Mister O'Malley. From this point on, you dumb-asses will not speak unless I ask you to! If you do, I'll hit you so hard, I'll knock your damn head down in your stomach so far you can watch your own self shit!"

That got our attention really fast. I was so quiet, I was afraid to even move my lips. There was no mistaking that I was in boot camp then.

We got off the bus and into a single-file line, standing there for about thirty minutes, until all the paperwork was signed. The cold wetness of February was blowing across the Chesapeake Bay. There I stood, in my overalls and two shirts, shivering in the cold and thinking "How long will he make us stand out here in this weather?"

Within a few minutes, Mister O'Malley marched us into a barracks. This was the start of Unit X. Anybody who ever went through boot camp in Norfolk will always remember Unit X. It was the place where they weeded out the weakest of the recruits. They kicked butt and took names there for a week before you went across the road to the rest of boot camp.

Mister O'Malley said, "I want you sorry-lookin', filthy, dirty, no-good civilians to take all your clothes off, put them in your suitcase or bags, and fill out this form, and then we are going to ship all your belongings back to your hometown. It won't cost you a penny. Uncle Sam will pay for us to ship everything back to wherever the hell you came from."

He looked at me and said, "Is this box all you have?"

"Yes, suh! I never owned no suitcase in my whole life."

"What have you got in this mile-long salt box?"

"Everything I own."

"Can I look inside?"

"Yes, suh!"

I untied the plow rope around the box and opened it up. Mister O'Malley looked inside. Boy, it was a sight to see. He told me, "That big, mile-long salt box won't be accepted at the post office. The mail people won't take it to ship back to your home. It's too fragile. Why don't you just walk over to that Navy trash can and put the whole damn thing in there? The Navy's gonna give you all the shoes, hats, underwear, work clothes, everything you need. They're going to really suit you up in about thirty minutes, after you get a shower."

I took my Miles Salt box over to the trash can and tossed it in, thinking, "Gee, that's everything I own; what am I gonna do?" I'd lugged the thing halfway across the United States with a bunch of old, beat-up clothes in it, but it was time for me to say good-bye to it. It was as though all my past went into that trash can with that Miles Salt box.

I got in line and took a shower. I had not had a bath in over a month. When I got out of the shower, I was handed a towel. As I'd soon find out, recruits who have been in basic training for a few weeks have to do a "service week". They hand towels and undershorts to the new recruits as they get out of the shower. After drying off, I put on my new undershorts and kept moving down the line as the Navy people were telling us what to do. "Move on, move your ass on down the line!" they kept yelling. That was all you could hear.

Each of us was issued a large canvas bag. "Here, sailor, here's your sea bag," they said as they handed us each one. We kept moving along this very long line, with other sailors putting things into our sea bags as we moved along. Handkerchiefs, socks, hats, and all kinds of stuff. We got four pairs of socks, four pairs of shorts, four T-shirts, one pair of dress shoes, and two pair of work shoes. At each station, I would stop and stare at these new clothes I was being given. It was more than I had ever had in my entire life.

A big bo'sun's mate—those were the big, tough guys in the Navy—grabbed me by the arm and threw me about ten feet.

"Goddamn it, you move yer cotton-pickin' ass down the line, and stop lookin' at every piece of clothes you git! Haven't you ever had any new clothes before?"

I got up off the floor, looked him straight in the eye, smiled and said, "Naw, suh!"

He kicked me in the ass and said, "Move your ass down and wipe that silly smile off your face!"

I moved along until my sea bag was full. Next, I was assigned to a barracks to sleep in, shown a mess hall where I would get three square meals a day, and get paid every two weeks, to boot. The whole time, I was thinking, "There's nobody gonna run my ass out of this organization! I've found a home, and by golly, I'm gonna stay here."

We had about thirty minutes after getting our sea bags filled before they started screaming at us again. During that half hour, my whole fourteen-year-old life ran through my mind. Sleeping alongside the road at night, no place to go; very little clothes to wear; wintertime without shoes; no family to take care of me; very little education. All this was running through my mind. I thought, "There is no sonofabitch big enough or bad enough to kick me out of this Navy. I'll do whatever it takes to stay the course."

We were marched into the base barbershop, where we each took a turn in one of the chairs. "You want your hair, boy?" the barber asked me when it was my turn.

"Yes, suh!" I said.

"Well, hold your hand out, 'cause here it comes!" He gave me the standard military buzz cut.

When I finally got into my bunk that night, I looked up to the ceiling and said, "Thank God, almighty, this boy's got shoes! Man, alive! My feet ain't never gon' get cold and turn blue again. Thank God, almighty, I got me some shoes!"

Glossary

battleships – A game boys played in the bayou where they rode cypress logs toward each other and tried to knock each other off.

bayou – another name for a slough in the delta, where the boys would fish, swim, etc.

bed tick – a sort of makeshift mattress, made of heavy canvas with a hole in the middle, stuffed with straw for summer and feathers for winter.

blackjack tree – a tree from which they took branches to brush their teeth when living in the log cabin.

boatswain's mate – (pronounced "BO-sun's mate"), petty warrant officer on a Navy ship.

cag – a keg; used for storing nails, then for sitting on.

calaboose – jailhouse.

carbide light – a lamp like a coal miner wears on his helmet; instead of a battery, it has a container into which carbide and water were put and sealed. It emits a gas through a small aperture in the container, which is lighted and reflects off the reflector at the back of the lamp to throw out a light.

chase chains – chains that ran from a wagon to the mules pulling it; they made a clanging sound as the wagon rolled.

churn – method of making butter from cream.

citaloid – a brown, plastic-like material similar to Bakelite.

coal oil lamp – kerosene lamp.

combine – (accent on the first syllable), a machine that threshes straw from the grain.

cook-off – where they make molasses from sorghum cane.

cow pond – a pond that was made from a dammed-up stream where the cows could drink in times of drought.

dewberries – wild berries found in the woods near the log cabin.

Feist – southern name for the rat terrier breed of dog.

finger-wave – Navy recruits' term for a digital rectal exam.

grip – a briefcase.

gumbo mud – thick, black mud that forms after heavy rains and flooding in the Mississippi delta.

jake-legging – a term used to refer to bootleggers who had gotten into some bad moonshine and had a problem with their legs; not complimentary.

lay-by time – the time when cotton is growing and doesn't require any work in the fields, usually about three to four weeks during the growing season.

maypops – lemon-sized fruits that grow wild on vines along the ground; when you step on a green one, it pops.

mother-in-law seat – a rumble seat on a car; it faced backwards and could be folded away when not in use.

muscadines – a type of grape that grew on Sand Hill near the log cabin.

mush – grits-like food enjoyed by Joe's grandfather.

nail cag – a nail keg; used for seating.

old-age pension – a state benefit offered to those who were elderly.

P&G – the letters on a bar of Octagon soap, made by Procter & Gamble; the kids said the letters stood for "Push & Grunt".

parch – roast, as in peanuts.

pea – a pear-shaped device on a hook that was moved to weigh cotton on a scale.

possum grapes – wild grapes that grew on Sand Hill near the log cabin; sweet, but eating them would give you diarrhea; used by Joe's mother for making wine.

private – penis.

river rats – in the Delta, people who lived along the levee.

sassafras tea – a root beer-like drink made from the roots of the sassafras bushes that grew wild in Mississippi.

sawmill gravy – a type of gravy made by Joe's mother and brother Dub to go with mush or fried cornbread.

school bus – a ton-and-a-half truck with a homemade bed that looked like a chicken coop, with benches down both sides and in the middle.

sea bag – a duffle bag issued to all Navy recruits for them to keep their belongings in when traveling.

seep waters – water that would seep through the levee in the delta at certain times, up to about ankle depth.

separator – a machine that separated milk from cream.

shock – (n.) a large pile of small, tied bundles of grain in the field. (v.) to group grain into such stacks.

slu – country spelling for a slough or bayou; a body of water where the boys would fish and play battleships.

smudge pot – a type of stove that often produces a lot of smoke, often used to protect plants from freeze; used as a heater on the covered wagon Joe rode to school in the bayou.

sorghum – a crop from which blackstrap molasses is made.

strippings – the last remnants of the cotton crop, after the first two pickings.

talkies – movies with sound.

toe sack – potato sack; a burlap bag.

trout line fishing – placing a line across a pond, with perpendicular lines every so far apart with baited hooks on them.

turkey chop – a type of bark emitted by a fox hound when in pursuit of a fox.

Victrola – a wind-up record player; stood about three feet high.

We Piddle Around – nickname for the Works Progress Administration, or WPA.

WPA – Works Progress Administration, a federal program started by President Franklin D. Roosevelt to give jobs to men who were unemployed during the Great Depression, while also getting roads, dams, etc. built.

Bibliography

Coben, Cy and Grean, Charles, "Sweet Violets", The New Novelty Songbook, Hal Leonard.

Dogomania website, "Feist / Rat Terrier". Cited 1/17/2005. www.dogomania.com.

Theodore Bilbo, Find A Grave Cemetery Records, cited 3/31/2005. http://secure.findagrave.com/cgi-bin/fg.cgi?page+gr&GRid=7134232&pt=Theodore%20Bilbo.

Mapquest website, cited on numerous dates. www.mapquest.com.

"Poverty's Palette, The Depression, in Kodachrome", The New York Times Magazine, May 9, 2004, pages 28-37.

Rand McNally Road Atlas, 1998 edition, Rand McNally Map & Atlas Division, Skokie, Illinois.

Timelines of History website, cited on numerous dates. http://timelines.ws.
Topek, Kevin, "Re: organic cherries". Ibiblio website, cited 10/13/2004. www.ibiblio.org/london/permaculture/mailarchives/permaculture-UNC/msg01192.html.

The Wheat Grower, September/October, 1994, as quoted on the Minnesota Association of Wheat Growers' website, cited 2/18/2005. www.smallgrains.org/whfacts/6CLASSWH.HTM.

(Footnotes)
1 From "Sweet Violets" by Cy Coben and Charles Grean, as published by Hal Leonard in The New Novelty Songbook, ©1951, renewed 1979.

LaVergne, TN USA
28 January 2011
214335LV00002B/129/P